THE WILLIAM JAMES LECTURES
Delivered at Harvard University, 1942–1943

MAN AND HIS WORKS

# Man and His Works

BY

EDWARD LEE THORNDIKE, *1874–1949.*

PROFESSOR EMERITUS, TEACHERS COLLEGE
COLUMBIA UNIVERSITY

WILLIAM JAMES LECTURER, 1942–1943
HARVARD UNIVERSITY

KENNIKAT PRESS, INC./PORT WASHINGTON, N. Y.

MAN AND HIS WORKS

Copyright 1943 by The President and
Fellows of Harvard College
Reissued 1969 by Kennikat Press by
arrangement with Harvard University Press

Library of Congress Catalog Card No: 69-16485
SBN 8046-0518-1
Manufactured in the United States of America

ESSAY AND GENERAL LITERATURE INDEX REPRINT SERIES

# PREFACE

THIS BOOK consists of the William James public lectures, given at Harvard University in the fall and winter of 1942, with almost no changes. The first three chapters present certain important facts about the original nature that is man's birthright, the laws of human modifiability or learning, and the human relations which influence man and his works. The other seven concern applications of psychology to the sciences of language, government, and philanthropy. Chapters IV to X, or any fraction of them, are intended to be intelligible even without the preparation given in Chapters I to III. I hope that students of language, political science, law, and sociology will find enough that is new in the appropriate chapters to make them profitable. I am sure they will be profitable to any thoughtful amateur in the sciences of man, if he can read them with interest; and I have tried to make them interesting.

EDWARD L. THORNDIKE

*Cambridge*
*January, 1943*

# CONTENTS

# MAN AND HIS WORKS

## THE ORIGINAL NATURE OF MAN:
## THE GENES OF THE MIND

FOR MANY THEORETICAL QUESTIONS about man and his works, and for many practical questions of education, government, business, and welfare, we need to know the abilities, wants, and proclivities that men have as the gift of nature, comparable to their eyes, teeth, and fingers. Nature's gifts to us come via the components of the fertilized ovum which is a man at his beginning, and especially via the genes, which are the components of the chromosomes in that fertilized ovum. The genes of snakes, dogs, chimpanzees, and men are probably alike in part, but they are certainly different in part. The genes which are influential in the development of the brains, minds, and behaviors of snakes, dogs, chimpanzees, and men differ as truly as do the genes which influence bodily forms.

We do not, however, know nature's gifts to men by direct examination of the human genes and their influences. We do not see the forces of nurture changing three fertilized human eggs into Smith, Jones, and Robinson. We have to infer what the contributions of heredity (that is, the genes) and of environment (that is, everything that acts upon the genes) are by indirect analyses.

The contributions of nature and nurture are much more readily distinguished in the case of animals like chicks which can be subjected to controlled environments. And a brief review of some of the facts for chicks is perhaps the best introduction to the facts and controversies concerning nature and nurture in man. It has also a certain appropriateness for these lectures since the observations to be reported were begun at Harvard, under the direction of William James.

The genes provide the chick with tendencies which, in its normal environment of a mother and a world of worms, seeds, dewdrops, etc., guarantee it a fair chance of life, liberty, and the pursuit of happiness. The mother serves chiefly as a stove, a guard against certain dangers, and an assistant in getting food. There is no reason to believe that her chicks learn anything from imitating her. They learn something from following her and obeying the calls she gives, but not very much. They get on very well without a mother if a warm shelter and a supply of edibles is provided.

The genes cause them to break their shell and climb out and away from it. The genes enable them to get food and drink, as truly as to digest it and turn it into bone and muscle and feather. Day by day as they grow the genes add to the chick's repertory of abilities and proclivities, and often in the form of complex and precise arrangements of what they feel and do in various situations. For example, the ability to perceive and react to distance, as in jumping down from a given height, is furnished in almost perfect form by the genes. At a given age a chick will, in order to get to food and companions, jump down from a height of 18 inches but not 28 inches, and at that age will jump down unconcernedly and at once from 15 inches, but after more delay and consideration from 18 inches, and after still more at 21 inches. The delicate connections in the brain whereby each inch of distance modifies the response are present in chicks that have never seen any creature jump down from anywhere. These connections change themselves day by day as directed from within the organism so that a chick fifteen days old will make jumps that a ten-day-old would refuse, though neither had ever jumped down from any height before.

A chick's first response to a dish containing milk or water or mush is directed by the genes, but not very usefully. The chick will, for example, walk in it or defecate on it, and will peck only at spots, bubbles, slight elevations, and the like. Why should we expect otherwise? The genes of a chick have no specific provisions for food or drink set forth in dishes! The specific heights from which a chick will jump are determined by the genes, but the specific objects at which a chick will eventually peck are selected from a wide variety by the course of the chick's learning. And the chick's genes provide responses to so general a situation as being alive and awake. In man too the genes provide connections leading from very specific situations, such as a tap below the knee, and also connections leading from so general a situation as being alive and awake rather than asleep.

As a rule the genes do not specialize where a general tendency, under the conditions of normal life and learning, will suffice. The precision of a chick or a child in getting small objects off the ground (or plate) into its mouth is not guaranteed by specific connections furnished by the genes. The finer adjustments desirable for small seeds, large seeds, worms, other soft pieces, cubes, circles, thin discs, etc., are selected by the forces of repetition and reward. It is the genes, however, that have given repetition and reward their potencies in the chick and in man.

The situations to which the genes provide responses may be very complex even in the chick. Solitary confinement evokes distinct and violent responses in chicks entirely apart from any previous experience. So does falling or being dropped into deep water — more exactly, finding oneself in a liquid medium with no solid support. Oddly enough, the chick's genes direct him to swim (or paddle, or run, as well as one can in the water) in a bee-line for the shore. A two-weeks old chick will thus cover ten feet in not many more seconds. No ancestor of the chick for millions of years has made much, if any, use of this talent, yet it has remained hidden in some napkin in the genes.

The human response to the same situation is much inferior. It would have been relatively easy for the genes to have kept a swimming response from our remote ancestors, or hooked in some kind of kicking or dog-paddling. But they have attached to the situation the response of grabbing at any solid object at hand, which is often worse for the man than doing nothing at all. This connection is a nuisance to rescuers, and a vice to be overcome in learning to swim. Note, however, that they have made better provision for falling through the air. Man then, as Darwin noted long ago, throws out his arms.

The genes of the chick link to many important features of its normal environment responses which are, or include, or can be modified by repetition and reward into, acts and attitudes more or less adequate to preserve the species. Within certain limits repetition and reward can adjust this repertory of connections to an abnormal or changed environment — to new and different situations. Thus a chick prevented by a wire screen or picket-fence from going directly to food, company, or other attractive object will, after unsuccessful efforts to push through or by, or fly over, the obstacle, go to the left and right and rear. If it thus makes a detour that brings escape and satisfaction, it will tend more strongly to make that detour at the next occurrence of that obstacle. Repetition and reward selecting from the tendencies provided by the genes or by earlier repetition and reward can teach it to respond to situation A by pulling a string, to situation B by stepping on a platform, to situation C by walking up stairs, to situation D by turning right, to situation E by turning left, to situation F by squeezing through a hole, and so on. If a proper environment is ingeniously provided a chick can be made to earn its living by choosing paths in mazes, operating mechanisms in puzzle boxes, and opening packages, though the mazes, mechanisms, and packages are as unknown to chick genes as alphabets, automobiles, and antitoxins are unknown to human genes. In general, the gifts of the genes are arranged to operate in an environment, preferably the expected environment, but as best they can in any environment. It is idle to expatiate, as some students of man do, upon this fact that original (that is, inherited or genetic) tendencies in man require the coöperation of certain environments to be effective. Every student of heredity knows it, and reckons with it.

In the case of chicks we can obtain a fair idea of the tendencies provided by the genes, and discover how in this, that, and the other environment they produce the total behavior of chicks. With sufficient study of a chick we should be able to predict its response to any situation, old or new, with a rather small margin or error. In the case of man we fall far short of this. If I should present an inventory of the original nature of man provided by his genes, it would be wofully incomplete, restricted in so many spots by "probably," "other things being equal," and "We do not know, but may conjecture," that it would be tiresome or irritating, or both, though exceedingly useful to the sciences of man. Also in spite of being incomplete, it would be very long. An inventory which I presented thirty years ago in *The Original Nature of Man* ran to several hundred pages; and many more items would now be added to that than subtracted from it.

Let us rather consider certain general facts about

man's gene equipment, and select such particular facts to illustrate them as will also give a just idea of what the total inventory would be like.

The first fact which I ask you to note is that there are probably thousands of genes influencing intellect, conduct, skill, and behavior; and that they certainly coöperate in thousands of ways. Human intellects differ from dogs' intellects largely by gene causation, but that does not mean that man has one "intellectual" gene, so to speak, which dogs lack, and which produces a differential in intellect directly, and independently of all other genes, and does nothing else.

Consider the unlearned or gene-caused features in what we call angry behavior.

(1) To the situation, "being interfered with in any bodily movements which the individual is impelled by its own constitution to make, the interference consisting in holding the individual," the little child makes instinctively responses of stiffening, writhing, and throwing back the head and shoulders. These are supplemented or replaced by kicking, pushing, slapping, scratching, and biting in the older.

(2) To a similar situation, with the difference that the interference is by getting in the way or shoving, the responses are: — dodging around, pushing with hands or body, hitting, pulling, and (though, I think, much less often) slapping, kicking, and biting.

(3) To the situation "being seized, slapped, chased or bitten (by any object) the escape-movements having been ineffective or inhibited for any reason," the fighting movements or the paralysis of terror may be the response.

To the particular situations that arise when attack provokes counter-attack, there are, I believe, particular responses. If A clings to B, trying to throw him down or bite him, B will, by original nature, more often try to push A away or throw him down than to hit or bite him. If A rushes at B, slapping, scratching, and kicking, B will, by original nature, more often hit and kick at A than try to push him away or throw him down. I believe that there is a basis in original nature for the distinction in sport between the fight with fists, which I judge to be a refinement (inappropriate as the word may seem) of the "slap-scratch-poke" fighting, and the wrestling match, which I judge to be a refinement of the "push-pull-throw-down-jump upon" fighting. When A and B are both down, the response is an effort to get on top. When A is beaten, it is originally satisfying to B to sit on him (or it), to stand exulting beside him (or it), and to remain unsatisfied until A has given signs of general submissiveness. Many other specialized original tendencies, such as to duck the head and lift up the arm, bent at the elbow, in response to the situation, "an object coming toward the head rapidly," appear in the course of a fight.

(4) To the situation "sudden pain" the response is attack upon any moving object near at hand. This fact, common in everyone's experience, may of course be interpreted as an acquired habit of response by analogy, but it seems to me that it is a true and beautiful case of nature's very vague, imperfect adaptations, which only on the whole and in a state of nature are useful. When a loving child with indigestion beats its mother who is trying to rock it to sleep (though it would protest still more if not rocked), or when a benevolent master punches the servant who is lifting his gouty foot, the contrary habits seem too strong to be overcome by the force of mere analogy with an acquired habit of hitting in response to the pain of actual conflict.

(5) To the situation, "an animal of the same species toward whom one has not taken the attitude of submis-

sion and who does not take it toward him" the human male responds by threatening movements, shoving the person away, and, if these fail to produce the attitude of submission, by either submission or further attack. The encounter is closed by the submission of either party, which may take place at any point.

(6) It seems probable also that to the situation, "the mere presence of a male of the same species during acts of courtship," the human male tends to respond by threatening or attacking movements until the intruder is driven away or the disturbed one himself flees.[1]

Besides these gross bodily responses, the genes connect flushing, snarling, a violent heart-beat, and the less easily observable responses within the brain which we are aware of as feelings of anger, with certain sorts of situations, and especially with the thwarting or frustration of any original tendency. All of these tendencies have, in my opinion, roots in the human genes, but I am equally certain that there is not one gene, nor one dozen genes, that produces all of them.

Scientific observations of infants show that the control of the body, from the wobbly searching movements of the head of the new-born to the locomotion and the digital explorations of many months later, and including raising the head, turning over from back to belly, turning from belly to back, reaching, grasping without the thumb, opposing the thumb, sitting up, standing up, squatting, and many scores of different performances, is instigated and directed in

[1] E. L. Thorndike, *The Original Nature of Man* (1913), pp. 68–73, *passim* and with minor changes.

large measure by the genes. The old notion was that nature gave only a miscellany of random movements any one of which was as likely to occur in any one situation as in any other situation, and that nurture slowly constructed adaptive movements out of these extensions, flexions, wiggles, waves, and spasms. On the contrary, a child gets these movements from the same source and with much the same regularity that it gets its teeth. They would probably suffice to move him adaptively in the normal environment of *Homo sapiens*. They serve as the materials out of which in the main even such "artificial" movements as the machinist's, or acrobat's, or pianist's, are created. There are scores, if not hundreds, of unlearned connections between various situations and these responses of bodily movement and posture.

I am confident that if the runnings, jumpings, embracings, chasings, wrestlings, squealings, chucklings, explorations with eyes and hands, manipulations destructive and constructive, and other behavior of babies and young children that we call play is carefully observed, much of it too will turn out to be based on a rather orderly repertory of scores of tendencies caused by the genes. Very little in it, in my opinion, is caused by selection from purely random acts. Very little in it (in my opinion nothing) is learned by a faculty of imitation in the sense of a tendency to make sounds as a result of hearing them made by man, and to make movements as a result of seeing them made by man.

As a final illustration of the extensive and elaborate

equipment for behavior provided as a gift of nature in the genes consider the responses to the behavior of persons. A child tends to be afraid when alone even though nothing harmful has ever occurred when he has been alone. He tends to run away from a human approaching him fast and to tag after a human departing from him slowly. He tends to move toward the point toward which others are moving and to run from the point whence they scatter. He tends to attack what the majority attack, and to flee from what puts them to flight. He is made happy by smiles, pats, and approving tones from those he esteems, disturbed by disregard, and wretched by scorn and derision. He plays the role of master when he can, and of vassal when he must or when the other person involved is of a size, energy, or natural impressiveness that makes submission natural and comfortable. These and other original connections of various acts and feelings with the behavior of fellowmen can be more or less altered, even reversed, by training, but training alone is hopelessly inadequate to account for them.

A second important fact to note is that the genes of *Homo sapiens* are not a fixed entity or collection always alike except for a few eccentric variations from one human type. On the contrary, "human type" is only a name for a very common collection among collections of genes that will produce men of entirely different heights, intellects, shapes of face, types of blood, color of skin, degrees of cheerfulness, etc., etc., grading down from prodigies of godlike men and women to monsters less acceptable as our mental and moral brothers than an average chimpanzee. Even in the number of teeth and fingers humanity does not guarantee identity. If it is true that man by original nature tends to enjoy sweet tastes more than bitter regardless of what he is fed, this does not mean that the original preference is equally strong in all men, or even that it may not be reversed in some men. Variation in behavior is not indicative of causation by environment, except in so far as the variations correspond to the expectancies from the said environments.

Per contra, if it were true that "every little boy or girl that is born into this world alive is either a little liberal or else a little conservative" it would not be proof that the genes include two allelomorphs of political preference! If a certain relevant feature of the environment is universal, universality need be no proof of gene origin. An interest in music of one sort or another is extremely common in man all over the world, but the provision for it in the genes probably is nothing more specific than a predilection to have one's neurones pleasantly active rather than idle, and a preference for rhythms over disorderly series. Tying the umbilical cord, giving each person a distinctive name, and burying the dead are perhaps now commoner than laughing when victorious, bringing objects caught or found to the mother for inspection, and leaping back convulsively when the hand unexpectedly touches a cold slimy object. But the former are nowise favored by the genes, whereas the latter are. When the habits inculcated by rewards given to various acts by life in a pastoral, agricultural, or machine age, or by tribal mores, are destroyed by brain disease, or lost in panic, tendencies may appear which training seems inadequate to account for, but which are strongly suggestive of the tendencies of our animal ancestors (we call them "beastly"). Though very rare in ordinary behavior, these may be determined by the genes. Freud has found it expedient, in order to explain man's life and work, to imagine a mob of selfish and devilish tendencies, called by him the ids. The ids are put under, and with difficulty kept under, by the top strata of the person, the ego and super-ego. In so far as the ids are real, they presumably come from the genes.

A third fact, known probably to all of you, is that the genes' equipment is not modified generation after generation by gaining a basis for tendencies acquired in life, or losing the basis for disused tendencies. There is no more inheritance of acquired traits in the case of mental abilities and proclivities than in the case of digestion or circulation. New genes may be added, but not from that source. Genes may be lost, but not for that reason. Training has no effect on the genes except in so far as it causes some persons and consequently some genes to have a greater expectation of life and more offspring than others. Literary men, and to some extent historians, have made such assertions as that many generations of nomadism, or pastoral life, or what not, left their impress on the natures of the Huns, or Semites, etc. The impress is on their institutions rather than their natures. The genes of a man stay just the same whether he lives in the mountains and valleys of Greece, or in the deserts of Arabia, whether he is a farmer or sailor, heathen or Christian, bond or free.

As a corollary to the absence of any inheritance of acquired traits, we have the fact that little or no adaptation to the productions of civilization during the past ten or twenty thousand years has occurred by additions to the genes. How much selection has done by killing off genetic strains less well adapted to using tools, tending flocks, growing plants, and working in factories, can only be conjectured. Within historical times its action seems to have been futile or even negative. On the whole it is reasonable to conclude that there are few or no genetically caused responses to domestic animals, plants, machines, factories, clothes, guns, vermin, filterable viruses, schools, churches, Buddhas, crucifixes, elections, democracy, etc., in man that were not available for the situations in question had they occurred to our ancestors of fifty thousand years ago.[2]

The next principle to consider is that the original tendencies to response set up by the genes are all limited to situations presented to the senses or represented to imagination as a consequence of presenta-

[2] We may perhaps assume that the genes of man provide behavior that is more or less adapted to the physical and social environmental normal for man a million or so years ago. But we know so little about what the environment then was, that this does not help us much.

tion to the senses. The genes, I am confident, provide no direct and primary responses to any mental images or ideas of concrete things, or judgments about them, much less to general or abstract ideas and judgments about them. For example, if the thought of being rich arouses joy, and the thought of being dead arouses anxiety, these connections have been fabricated by training. A man will by original nature struggle long against confining bonds and rejoice greatly at being released to unimpeded movement, but he will not by original nature alone move a hair's breath at the judge's sentence to imprisonment, or the warden's news of a pardon.

This is important, if true. Statements about man's religious instincts, political instincts, instinctive love of security, flattery, or domination, instinctive fear of death, danger, or disrepute, and many others often imply the contrary, and encourage us to expect from nature much that she does not give. Stock descriptions of the religious instinct, for example, set forth that man, beset by events that he cannot understand, imagines supernatural persons or forces and responds to these by awe, sacrifice, prayer and the like. My contention is that the only power that these imaginations of man, or revelations to man, have by original nature rests in their resemblances to things, qualities, or events perceptible to the senses. Much of their power they acquire by indirect links of association. Some of man's responses to his deities are as remote from the genes as his responses to sines, cosines, and differential equations are. Psychiatrists assert that man by nature seeks security, and their assertions are interpreted to mean that the genes give man a predilection for unemployment insurance, old-age pensions, and paternalistic government. The security which the genes cause men to seek is in such concrete sensed forms as a mother's arms, a snug little cave, a full stomach, or an encircling friendly human group.

As a last example we may take the allegedly natural cravings for life, liberty, and the pursuit of happiness, whereby man acts to preserve his mundane existence, rebels against all tyrannies and restraints, and behaves very much like a composite of the economic man and the average *homme sensuel* of the French philosophers. Psychology teaches that, on the contrary, such a man is an advanced and artificial product far removed from the man the genes produce. The latter seeks life only to the extent of running from such-and-such sensed objects, selecting or constructing natural lairs, etc. He values liberty only in the sensory forms of freedom to move unthwarted, go where he likes, eat what he finds, etc. It is over a long road of training that he comes to have the ideas of life and death, liberty and slavery, welfare and misery.

Man has been defined as the tool-using animal, and the genes provide tendencies of manipulation, curiosity, and pleasure at making something happen by one's activities. These tendencies, together with certain intellectual powers, can cause man to use sticks, stones, bones, shells, etc., as tools and to improve them for their work. They did in fact in the course of time cause man to do so. But very few tool-using activities appear full-fledged as a gift of nature. They have a basis in the genes, but develop only if and when certain additional forces are furnished by the experiences of life.

Man is everywhere the speaker, and the faculty of speech has been credited to the genes by many. Even Boas, who in general is very averse to relying on the genes, says "The faculty of speech is organically determined and should be called therefore, instinctive." [3] This is in a sense true, but is likely to mislead. The causation is complex, being somewhat as follows: Man by nature moves the tongue and other mouth parts to produce a great variety of sounds, and has pleasure in doing so. These movements, in connection with certain intellectual powers, can produce meaningful speech, and language as an elaborate and flexible communicative art. But it is not at all certain that they *must* do so. Men with genes like ours may have lived for hundreds of generations with little more language than the monkeys — with, for example, no words for eat, drink, mother, friend, yes, no, red, white, green, hot, cold, one, or two. They may have invented language as they invented tools of flint. A human family without language would seem hardly human in behavior, but its genes might be identical with ours.

These intellectual powers, that turn manipulative play into constructive techniques and create meaningful speech out of prattling, account also for many other important traits and achievements of man.

[3] *Anthropology and Modern Life* (1928), p. 136.

They have been essential in the creation of the environment of axes, arrows, and traps, domesticated animals, cultivated plants, huts, rafts and boats, controlled heat and light, speech, writing, customs and traditions, on to the latest machine-gun, vaccine, vitamin, airplane, encyclopedia, and law. They produce changes in the material, social, and intellectual environment which react to produce changes in the intellectual powers, forming on the whole a beneficent circle, whose story is the story of civilization. At our next meeting I shall present a simple and, I hope, a true explanation of them.

For our present hour, it remains to note man's love of sensory experience and motor activity for their own sake, and his love of power over things and thoughts for its own sake. A human child wants sights and sounds and touches regardless of their value as means to food or safety. Experience, especially novel experience, is its own sufficient reward. The child also wants muscular activity for activity's sake. Exploration and manipulation which satisfy these wants are almost incessant occupations of our waking infancy. The genes of man seem to provide many neurone connections besides those concerned in surviving, getting food, getting a mate, and aiding a second generation to do the same. And these neurone-connections seem as ready to act as any others. Such connections operate and give marked satisfaction at a level above or beyond that of simple sensory experience or simple motor play, on the level of mental control or "doing something to make something happen." A baby likes to see blocks tumble when he hits them, and to hit them with the expectation of seeing them fall. The same general fact and principle appears at a level still more remote from mere sensory experience and motor play, in the field of images and ideas, and thought with words. As soon as the child gets mental images he plays with them, and is satisfied thereby. As soon as he has words and thoughts he plays with them, and is satisfied thereby. And, in general, unforced and unthwarted mental activity going on under a man's control is as natural to man as hunting or eating.

The contributions of the genes to the behavior which I have been describing in the last five minutes are their great and distinctive gifts to man. They, more than all else, make him man. A great increase in intellectual capacity and a great increase in the variety of manual, vocal, and intellectual play are the main genetic bases for man's achievements.

## II

### MODIFICATION BY THE ENVIRONMENT:
### LEARNING

A GOOD SIMPLE DEFINITION or description of a man's mind is that it is his connection system, adapting the responses of thought, feeling, and action that he makes to the situations that he meets.

A man's original nature, carried by the fertilized egg that is the man at his beginning, causes him to connect many sensations, feelings, and acts with many situations or events, as noted at our first meeting. But a large percentage of the connections that operated in you during, say, the last week were caused, as you know, by the environment in which you have lived and learned, and would have been very different if your genes had been born ten thousand years ago in Central Africa.

At this meeting we are to examine these acquired connections — these additions to, and modifications of, the original gene-caused stock.

A description of a person as of a given moment would consist of a list of all the situations that he might possibly encounter and be sensitive to and lists of all the responses that he might possibly make to each, and statements of the probability that any of the situations would evoke any of the responses in that person. Using S for any situation or state of affairs or fact in nature to which the man is or could become sensitive, and R for any thought, feeling, act, or whatever else a man can be or do, we could describe a man approximately by a list of some billions of S's, each of which would be accompanied by a short or long list of R's, with the probability P that the S in question would evoke the R in question. The P's would range from near 1.00 or surety, as in the case of the response of one of you to the total situation of this moment as I ask you to think of the sum of 5 and 2, down to infinitesimals, as in the case of the probability that to this same situation and question the response should be, in one of you, not the thought of seven, but the thought of a four-horned rhinoceros. The bulk of a mind is a set of routines, but there is a fringe of small probabilities that has almost infinite extent. The situations in the form of distinguishable human faces and signatures alone would surely exceed a million, and these must all be multiplied by the number of possible backgrounds on which each face or signature might appear. And, in general, the number of situations with which a person might be confronted and to which he might be sensitive is practically infinite.

However, there is no other way of truly describing a person at any one moment of his life; and no way of truly describing a person over a period of time save by combining the facts for each moment of it. Any given person is what he will think and feel and do in various circumstances. He is the probabilities that each of the R's that he can produce will be evoked by each of the S's that can evoke anything from him. He is the total of his S→R probabilities. It is by adding to these S→R connections, and by changing the probability of one or another of them up or down, that the environment changes him.

These statements are true, quite irrespective of the truth of a connectionist psychology. They are true for those who still believe in the old faculty psychology. Whatever the faculties of perception, attention, imagination, reasoning, and the rest accomplished they accomplished by influencing probabilities that certain S's would evoke certain R's. They are true for those who believe in the Gestalt psychology. If "insight," "closure," etc., produce any results, their results will appear as changes in these S→R probabilities. They are true for adherents to a "hormic" psychology. When a purpose does anything in a man, its fruits must appear in these probabilities.

The kind of psychology which is called connectionist or, less attractively, Thorndikian, differs from these others in the forces that it uses to account for the development of the infinitely rich, elaborate, and complex array of S→R probabilities which a human mind is. It uses only two, which we will for the present call *repetition* and *reward*. Better names will be given to them after we have presented certain facts about them.

They are the only forces which I shall use in any of these lectures to account for anything in man's work. To those of you who are students of psychology it should be of special interest to see how well one can explain, for example, the origin of language by the action of these two simple forces upon certain gene-given connections. And those of you whose chief interest is in language or government or welfare will, I hope, find some interest and profit not only in our general study of these as products of human minds, but also in the causation by these two simple forces of results which you have previously been led to expect required imitation, suggestion, configuration, insight, tensions, ids, egos, or more mysterious potencies.

The force which I just called repetition is properly named occurrence, since even one occurrence never repeated has some power. It is properly named the occurrence of a response to a situation, because occurrences of a situation make no change in a man unless they lead to some response by him, and because occurrences of a response by a man are in the nature of the case associated with some situation, if only that of being alive. The word "to" is important. When one responds to the situation "What is the square of 10?" by writing, saying, or thinking "100," the 100 clearly "belongs to" the "What is the square of 10?", is evoked by it, and presumably is physiologically linked to it as a later part of some neural activity of which the earlier part represents the question. This belonging and physiological linkage may be present to some extent, however, when the response has no important fitness or relevance to the situation. Indeed a response that is primarily to "What is the square of 10?" may also to some degree be to anything and everything that is happening in the mind or brain of the person at the time.

In some cases the probability that a certain situation will evoke a certain response cannot be increased by either repetition or reward. Some functions are exempt from learning; some others have reached a physiological limit. In the great majority of cases, however, every occurrence of a response to a situation increases the probability that that situation will, if it recurs, evoke that response. Most of you if now asked to write within a second or two the square of 27 will have a very low probability of writing 729. But if you do so with my guidance as I say 27 squared 729, 27 squared 729, 16 squared 256, 18 squared 324, 27 squared 729, 15 squared 225, 16 squared 256, 27 squared 729, 19 squared 361, 18 squared 324, 27 squared 729, 16 squared 256, 16 squared 256, 27 squared 729, 19 squared 361, 15 squared 225, 16 squared 256, most of you will be able to write the correct square of 27 now within the second. The probability of that response to that situation within that time has risen from near zero to near 1.00, i.e. surety, for the time being.

The customary name for a response linked to a situation is a mental connection. And the customary statement of the fact that the occurrence of a response R to a situation S increases the probability that S will if it recurs, evoke R is that the occurrence of the connection S→R strengthens or reinforces that connection. More exactly, the occurrence of the connection S→R in a person P in a certain state, St, strengthens the tendency of that person in that state to respond to S by R. To form a mental connection S→R is to raise the probability from zero to some substantial amount. To weaken a connection is to decrease the probability that the S in question will evoke the R in question. By enough occurrences the probability that "What is the square of 27?" will evoke 729 could be put above surety in the sense that it would not only be sure to evoke it in the present but also in the distant future. The mental connection could become so strong as to maintain itself against the weakening influence of lapse of time or the operation of competing connections.

But unless you welcomed such bits of mathematical knowledge, this would require many occurrences. An unrewarded occurrence may add little to the strength of a mental connection.[1] "What is the square of 16?" Some of you cannot at once tell, though only a few minutes ago you had five occurrences of "16 squared 256," which, however, had little or no interest for you. The influence of the experiences of life upon a person's mind is largely by way of occurrences to which a reward is attached.

By a reward is meant satisfyingness to the person in question at or very soon after the occurrence. By the force of reward is meant the fact that, if a certain response is made to a situation with resultant satisfaction accompanying or closely following it then and there, the probability that that response will be

---

[1] I say may because in the case of genuine Pavlovian modification of reflexes, sheer occurrence may have special potency.

made to that situation if it recurs is increased, and increased more than it would be by an unrewarded occurrence. Or, in more usual terms, mental connections are strengthened by satisfying accompaniments or after-effects.

Such potency of satisfyingness involves a sort of teleological causation, and requires that something that takes place after a connection has operated work back upon the connection to strengthen or reinforce it. Consequently psychology has been loath to believe in any such potency of satisfyingness. On the one hand there has been reliance upon mere repetition (that is, occurrence). On the other hand there has been recourse to mysterious tendencies toward "equilibrium," or the relief of "tension," or upon the dominance of the connection that ends in a "consummatory response." But experiments made during the past decade have proved that the after-effects of a connection do in fact work back upon it, and have shown how the teleological causation in question can be consistent with, and a part of, natural biological causation.

One of these experiments is so instructive that I shall take the time to report it to you. First let me demonstrate a crude form of it as a group experiment. Each of you has a record sheet with 135 spaces in each of which you will write a number — 1 or 2 or 3 or 4 or 5. I hold in my hand a list of 135 words, each followed by a number (1 or 2 or 3 or 4 or 5). I shall read the word aloud, but read the number to myself only. Many of the words occur two or three times on my list. Every time a word appears it is followed by the same number. You will write 1 or 2 or 3 or 4 or 5 just as soon as you hear each word. Begin at the top of the first column and go down. Sometimes I shall inform you whether the number you have written is the number that belongs with the word by saying "One is right" or "Two is right," or the like. Sometimes I shall not. The first time you hear any word you will obviously have to just guess or use whatever telepathic abilities you have. So also for the next time you hear it, unless I have given information the first time. You need not make any special effort to remember the information that I gave. Let this experiment be a pleasant relaxation. I will however report to you whether you showed any notable telepathic power and also how well you profited from the information that I gave, if you will write your name and address on the record sheet. The only requirements of you are (1) that you fill each space from 1 to 135 with a number (1 or 2 or 3 or 4 or 5), (2) that you write the number immediately after I say the word, and before I give any information about which number was "right" or say the next word. If for any reason you failed to write a number in time, make a dash so as to keep your place. I cannot send you a true record unless your entries on the record sheet match my readings.

[The experimenter then read as follows at a rate of about 2½ seconds per item, using 5 minutes 30 seconds in all.]

1. wax 5 is right
2. tunnel 4 is right
3. oak
4. noble
5. artist
6. select
7. dragon 3 is right
8. vest
9. original
10. bishop
11. twins 2 is right
12. pen
13. nervous 5 is right
14. unfold
15. golden
16. map
17. reply 2 is right
18. evening 1 is right
19. tug
20. dry
21. hopeless
22. drug 3 is right
23. wag
24. lovely 4 is right
25. allow
26. nickel 5 is right
27. Sunday
28. horrible
29. expose
30. wig
31. passage
32. fisherman 2 is right
33. outside
34. army
35. bank 5 is right
36. mix 1 is right
37. chatter
38. square 4 is right
39. reduce
40. ignore
41. wish
42. boundary
43. float 2 is right
44. shadow 3 is right
45. unity 1 is right
46. rope
47. punish 4 is right
48. artist
49. select
50. dragon 3 is right
51. vest
52. original
53. bishop
54. twins 2 is right
55. pen
56. nervous 5 is right
57. unfold
58. golden
59. map
60. reply 2 is right
61. evening 1 is right
62. tug
63. dry
64. hopeless
65. drug 3 is right
66. wag
67. lovely 4 is right
68. allow
69. nickel 5 is right
70. Sunday
71. horrible
72. expose

73. wig
74. passage
75. fisherman 2 is right
76. outside
77. army
78. bank 5 is right
79. mix 1 is right
80. chatter
81. square 4 is right
82. reduce
83. ignore
84. wish
85. boundary
86. float 2 is right
87. shadow 3 is right
88. unity 1 is right
89. dog
90. artist
91. select
92. dragon 3 is right
93. vest
94. original
95. bishop
96. twins 2 is right
97. pen
98. nervous 5 is right
99. unfold
100. golden
101. map
102. reply 2 is right
103. evening 1 is right
104. tug

105. dry
106. hopeless
107. drug 3 is right
108. wag
109. lovely 4 is right
110. allow
111. nickel 5 is right
112. Sunday
113. horrible
114. expose
115. wig
116. passage
117. fisherman 2 is right
118. outside
119. army
120. bank 5 is right
121. mix 1 is right
122. chatter
123. square 4 is right
124. reduce
125. ignore
126. wish
127. boundary
128. float 2 is right
129. shadow 3 is right
130. wax
131. tunnel
132. oak
133. noble
134. rope
135. punish

I know from many experiments that the majority of even so sophisticated a group as this have an appreciable satisfaction at being right in even so unim-

portant a matter as learning the number belonging
to a word. But for safety's sake let us check this by
asking those who did not feel any more satisfied
when they were right than when they were wrong or
left in doubt to rise.[2]

Let us check further. By putting the question as
I did, I had shyness and indolence in favor of my
expectation. So will those please rise now who *did*
feel more satisfaction when they were right than
when they were wrong or left in doubt.[3]

If, now, we should examine the records of those to
whom success was satisfying we should find that in
general satisfying connections were strengthened
more than the others. But with that we are not now
concerned. What we are now concerned with is that
we should find also that the connections that were
near to a rewarded connection were strengthened
more than those that were remote from it. For example, the situation "dragon write a number" occurred as number 7 and again as number 50, and a
third time as number 92. It was preceded by "select"
as 6 and 49 and 91, and was followed by "vest" as 8
and 51 and 93. If you wrote 3, the connection was
rewarded, and if we should study what happened to
the connections you made we should find that you
tended not only to repeat the rewarded connection
dragon→3 much more than chance would account
for, but also to repeat whatever connections you made
with "select" and "vest" somewhat more than chance

[2] No one in the audience rose.
[3] Over nine-tenths of the audience rose.

and mere occurrence would account for. The reinforcement influences chiefly dragon→3 but also spreads or scatters to neighboring connections. In an experiment much like the one you have shared in, connections next to a rewarded connection were repeated in the next round of the series in 24 per cent of the cases, whereas connections remote from any rewarded connection (with four or more words between) were repeated in only 21 per cent of the cases.[4]

In 1932 and 1933 I made many experiments of this general nature to see whether the influence of a satisfying after-effect would not only strengthen notably the connection to which it was attached, but also spread or scatter to strengthen somewhat neighboring connections. It always did; and my results were soon confirmed by other workers here and in Europe.

This spread or scatter phenomenon has a two-fold importance. First, it is a crucial test of the general hypothesis that satisfying consequences of a connection can work back upon it, since here they work back even beyond it to a preceding connection and one which produces no equilibrium, relieves no tension, and consummates nothing. Second, it suggests that the strengthening by satisfying consequences

[4] In the experiment made at the lecture, connections next to a rewarded connection were repeated in the next round of the series in 34 per cent of the cases, whereas those remote from any rewarded connection (with four or more words between) were repeated in the next round in only 30 per cent of the cases.

may have a biological causation nearly as simple as that which gives repeated occurrences their power. Perhaps all that is required is that the over-all control of a person or animal (what we used to call the "higher" centers) should be able to react to a certain stimulus by a reinforcement of whatever connection has most recently been active, and that the stimulus that sets off this "confirming reaction" should be satisfying to the over-all control.

The probability that a certain response will be made to a situation would then be a function, first, of the number of times it has been made to that situation and second, of the number of times it has been hit, so to speak, by the confirming reaction.

A mental connection strengthens itself by occurring; it is also strengthened when the confirming reaction impinges upon it. This confirming reaction may be as simple an affair physiologically as being awake rather than asleep, or being at peace rather than afraid.

The confirming reaction acts biologically, not logically. It does not pick out infallibly the connections which the person wishes to strengthen, and confirm, that is, strengthen, them. It strengthens primarily the connection that has just been acting, but may strengthen a neighboring connection in addition or instead. It acts more like a hormone than like a syllogism. Also it does not vary in close correspondence with the amount of satisfiedness of the person. Experiments by Rock have shown that increasing the amount of the reward from a mere statement of "right," to such a statement plus a gift of one or two

units of money, or from the latter to the statement
plus a gift of three or four units of money, make little
or no difference in the potency of one rewarded
occurrence to raise the probability that the situation
in question will evoke the response in question. The
rise above chance caused by "right" alone averaged
18; that for "right" plus one or two units of money
averaged 17; that for "right" plus three or four units
of money averaged 19. The confirming reaction is
more like the knee jerk than like either a syllogism or
a cash register.

The confirming reaction is not held in reserve for
great affairs, exciting emergencies, and decisive
choices. You do not have a dozen a week, or a dozen
a day, but more nearly a dozen a minute. To each
phrase that I speak you respond by a certain meaning. If this meaning satisfies you by making sense,
the connection is confirmed. Similarly, in reading a
page a satisfying flow of sense is confirmed step by
step. But if difficulty or confusion arises, the confirming reaction is withheld and one or another
change in your responses may be tried until you
reach a status that is tolerable.

Millions of such confirmations of your interpretations of speech and reading from the time you were a
year old till today have largely caused your present
understanding of language. In the handling of knife
and fork and spoon, pen and pencil, toys and tools,
sensori-motor connections have been confirmed from
moment to moment, and the confirming reaction has
thus largely caused your present skills.

The reinforcement of the just active connection is

not limited to "little" and clean-cut connections like "5 + 2 equals 7," "French oui = English yes," "pusillanimity means a kind of cowardliness," "tap the typewriter here for s and there for t," but applies to "large" trends and total thoughts. In fact anything which may be connected with anything in the mind may be more strongly connected therewith by the confirming reaction. The situation may be and often is a pattern rather than an object. So a seen word *s a t* may have a certain sound connected with it regardless of whether it is in type covering a fiftieth of a square inch or in type covering five times that area, in black ink or blue ink or red ink. A mind can respond to ratios and other relations and be confirmed in its responses to such. The response may be an emotion or an attitude. For example, if you like the look of a certain combination of colors and then and there find your liking shared by friends of esteemed esthetic judgment, you will be more likely to like it the next time than you will be if you then and there find your liking commiserated or scorned. We can by suitable training measurably increase a schoolgirl's liking for gold on Christmas cards and measurably increase her distaste for silver on such cards. And the training consists in confirming these tendencies by such comments by the experimenter for the liking of cards with gold, as: — "Yes! A very attractive picture," "Yes, it is attractive to artists," "Yes, I like it too"; and, for the disliking of cards with silver, by such comments as: — "Yes, it's a mess," or "Yes! Most people of good taste consider it poor," or "Yes! I wonder who buys atrocities like that."

We know more about what the confirming reaction does than about what issues it. But we know something about that. I have said that it has its source in the over-all control of a person at the time. This over-all control may be any one of the numerous selves of a man. If he is playing tennis his tennis-playing self is in command; good strokes and points won are satisfiers; failures to hit the ball and feeble pokes at it are annoyers. If he is eagerly learning Latin, knowing the meanings of words and correct translations of sentences are satisfiers to him as translator and to the deeper self that will feel enriched and dignified by being a better Latin scholar.

In some cases a very large fraction of a person shares in the issuance of the confirming reaction. So a person choosing a career will bring more of himself to bear upon the flow of his thought than a person writing a Limerick or polishing his shoes. The case is conceivable, though hardly realizable in any actual man, where all of the person except the two terms whose linkage is strengthened issues a confirming reaction that acts upon that linkage.

At the other extreme a case is conceivable in which nothing more of a person than a single minor want or purpose has any direct share in the confirmation. Some real cases approach such narrowness. Thus a person utterly obsessed by his search for a rhyme for *illustrate* might push away a call to dinner, a ten-dollar bill, and a brilliant idea about preventing wars, in favor of *frustrate*.

The confirming reaction has its origin outside the situation→response unit upon which it acts, whereas the strengthening by mere occurrence presumably has its origin inside it. In what physiological events the strengthening consists is unknown in both cases. Strengthening from without by a confirming reaction may be an accentuation of the same kind of physiological event as represents strengthening from within by mere occurrence; or it may be by an addition of something different.

It should be noted here that there is no simple opposite of the confirming reaction — no efflux or message from the over-all control that weakens the mental connections upon which it impinges. Nature might have provided man with a tendency for annoying, diswanted after-effects to evoke from the over-all control something that would everywhere decrease probabilities of recurrence as much as the confirming reaction increases them. But there is no such tendency. Pains, frustrations, and other annoyers are potent in man's life, but not at all by a reverse action to that of satisfiers. On the contrary a punished S→R occurrence, that is, one in which the S→R has an annoying after-effect, like the announcement "wrong," or the announcement "wrong" plus a sharp electric shock, usually gains more strength by occurring than it loses by being so punished. In the ordinary course of his learning man modifies himself, not by weakening his undesired tendencies absolutely by punishing them but only by weakening them relatively by strengthening competing tendencies.

What pains, frustrations, and other annoyers do

do and how they do it would make a long story, some
of which I may relate in the lectures on government.
Very briefly, they seem to influence human modification beneficially only by their associations with
fear, shame, and the like, or by leading the person to
replace the undesirable connection by a desirable
one and to reward that.

The general consequences of the action of reward
are very different from those assumed by the pleas-
ure-pain psychology of Bentham, Spencer, Bain, or
their followers. Human beings are not propelled by
pleasure and repelled by pain in any such uniform
ways as these hedonists assumed. Psychologists have
long realized that they are not, and we can now see,
at least in part, why they are not, and what does the
work that they were invoked to do. Pleasures do
ordinarily act as satisfiers, but they need not. To a
fanatic convinced that a certain delight was sent by
the devil to destroy his soul, any connection that
brought a thrill of that delight would excite no confirming reaction. When pleasurable consequences do
strengthen the connections that produce them, the
amount of the pleasure beyond a certain minimum
required to set off a confirming reaction is of very
little influence. Pain is only one of the annoyers, the
diswanted events in life. It is not dynamically a true
opposite of pleasure.

The confirming reaction may be in some cases the
act of a free agent, a free will, in the most useful sense
of those words. Science hitherto has denied this or
seemed to deny it. Science commonly thinks of the

modifications in human beings as caused by the environment, including the social environment constituted by other living men and the intellectual and moral environment constituted by all the surviving institutions of men living or dead. The environment, in this very broad sense of the world with all its persons, customs, arts, religions, and sciences, undoubtedly determines most of what occurs in a man and most of what is rewarded. Most, but not all.

To some extent a man modifies himself. The confirming reaction is issued by a man when that man is satisfied. That man originates as a certain collection or battery or outfit of genes which is by definition and hypothesis apart from and contrasted with its environment. Day by day that man has changed his nature partly by the influence of his own confirmations of connections whose consequences satisfy him. Each person is to that extent an *imperium in imperio naturae*. Each person is a center of creative force, modifying himself more or less to suit himself.

A fraction of mental causation is thus teleological. If the confirming reaction does not give us a teleology, it gives us something better. A man's purposes largely control what satisfies him. The consequences of a tendency largely decide its future history. Rewarded occurrences become reoccurrences, and eventually habits. The sciences of government, law, economics, business, education, and morals have assumed that human nature had some arrangements whereby people could choose their lines of action, do what they wanted to do rather than what they wanted not to do, seek their own advantage or that of some other person, and in other ways be pulled by ideas and purposes as well as pushed by events. The confirming reaction will give them, I prophesy, all that they need.

Yet there is nothing supernatural or extranatural about it. It is as natural a biological fact as pleasure or pain or sleep. We may hope to discover the mechanism that causes a man to issue a confirming reaction as well as the mechanisms that make him feel pleasure or fall asleep.

# III

## HUMAN RELATIONS

As an introduction to today's discussion I ask you all to engage in a little introspection, as follows: Suppose that you are sitting on your doorstep and a certain man comes up and greets you. Consider the differences in how you would think and feel and act, according as your relation to the man is that of:

(1) employer to employee
(2) employee to employer
(3) doctor to patient
(4) patient to doctor
(5) salesman to customer
(6) customer to salesman

The man is to be the same person in all six cases, as nearly as is possible.

These are samples from a long list of relations in which the same two persons might find themselves, including teacher to pupil, pupil to teacher, host to guest, guest to host, lender to borrower, ruler to subject, master to servant, owner to slave, friend to friend, enemy to enemy, representative to voter, pastor to parshioner, stranger to stranger, protector to protected, leader to led.

These relations are rightly called political, legal, economic, etc., and dealt with by the sciences of sociology, government, law, economics, business, and education. But they are also essentially psychological, being determined by human nature as well as by human institutions.

Consider as a sample the relation of seller and buyer. As a purely economic fact we have a seller who prefers a certain amount of money ($M_1$) to the continued ownership of certain commodities, and a buyer who prefers the ownership of said commodities to the ownership of a certain amount of money ($M_2$). If $M_2$ equals or exceeds $M_1$, a sale occurs with a net gain in satisfaction to seller, or buyer, or both. When the seller has used the money to buy, the two sales with money as a medium of exchange equal one barter. By billions of sales each week the individuals of the world barter things they want less for things they want more.

But the purely economic features of a sale are not the whole fact. The fact of freedom to buy and sell, that is, that any person who has the money can become the owner of the commodity, and vice versa, is one of the genuinely just and democratic facts in our world. In so far as my dollar will get for me what any other man's dollar will get for him, I can feel that the world is just.

The fact that as buyer or seller I have power enables me to feel more content with myself. This is especially true of the position of buyer. The seller of wheat, cotton, or sugar has power only over the few who want wheat or cotton or sugar more than money. But the buyer can habitually use his money to command anybody who has anything to sell.

A woman on a shopping trip can be the master of all sellers whom she surveys, a monarch on a tour of triumph. She does in fact command deference, not to say subservience. So the credo of the modern department stores affirms that the customer is always right. So the iron hand of the salesman must wear the velvet glove. Even the shy and timorous college professor who is buying a present for his wife, and who is really as wax or putty in the saleslady's hands, is made to feel that he is master of the situation. If some clerk violates these unwritten laws, it will usually suffice to remind him, "You are *behind* the counter."

Between the lowest price which the seller is willing to take and the highest price that the buyer is willing to give there is, in case a sale can be made to the advantage of both, a margin ranging from zero or near zero up to substantial amounts. The division of this margin may become the subject of a trading battle, offer entertainment as a contest, and bring into action the cravings to show one's bargaining skill, and to be, or at least think oneself, the winner. The training in concealing one's own condition and discerning the other party's condition may encourage habits of bluffing and other forms of deceit. It may arouse greedy or generous impulses and behavior. The greedy impulses may distort trading contests into the exercise of what Marshall has called "the miserable ingenuity" of a "laborious astuteness in bargaining, on which people with small capitals, and especially agriculturists, in all countries often lay stress: priding themselves on their skill in buying a thing for less than it is worth, and selling a thing for more than it is worth." [1] It may arouse suspicion, as in the farmer who, when offered a price much above the market for a pile of firewood, refused in these words, "If it's worth that to you I guess it's worth that to me."

There has been a specialization and division of the relations in which a man stands to his fellow men comparable to the specialization and division of labor. But the specialization of human relations has not narrowed and stereotyped the man's social activities as the specialization of labor has narrowed his activity as producer. On the contrary, the American worker who, on the assembly line in his factory, performs a very few operations, has added to the relations of family, neighborhood, church, etc., which a man of his ability and rank would have had in medieval times many new ones — relations to his union, his lodge or club, his political party, his ward leader, his movie favorite, his radio stars, announcers, and commentators, his heroes in baseball, in the prize-ring, and the comics, and, indeed, all the persons and nations that figure in his daily paper.

There is a different sort of specialization which is caused by psychological facts of great importance. Consider as an example the relation of co-worker to co-worker in an enterprise. We use the words coöperation and coöperativeness, but the relation has hundreds of forms varying with the nature of the

[1] A. Marshall, *Industry and Trade* (1920), p. 47.

enterprises, the ways in which they are conducted, and the persons with whom one has to coöperate. A dozen pick-and-shovel men under a foreman coöperate by keeping out of one another's way, pushing together to turn over a big stone, and the like, all under direction. The eleven men on a football team should coöperate by each doing his task in the routines of a complex play, and, what is harder and beyond the abilities of many, by quickly selecting the helpful action to perform in an emergency in view of what the others are doing. Members of a farmer's coöperative organization for selling have to coöperate mainly by the simple moral acts of living up to their agreements with each other as to quality of goods and restriction of sales. Sheer dishonesty ruined coöperatives formed by the Southern tobacco farmers in the '20's. Lindeman, who was an ardent sympathizer with them and their purposes, reports that 38 per cent of a coöperative group had sold portions of their product in violation of their contract. The coöperation of the staff of a railroad in doing its work includes all these kinds of physical, intellectual, and moral coöperation and many more. It, like most industrial coöperation, works with the aid of an elaborate system of signals, messages, orders, reports, expert services of accountants and technologists, all organized under the management, so that each of ten thousand men coöperates with thousands whom he never sees, and about whose work he knows almost nothing. But there can also be nearly a maximum of coöperation with nearly a minimum of system. Such is the case with coöperation in the discovery of truth by men of science. Each does what he thinks best to do, and is related to the rest only via their published accounts of their work and occasional conferences and correspondence.[2]

Coöperativeness is similarly mutifarious and specialized. It is not a simple and unitary trait varying only in amount like length or weight, of which some persons possess much and other persons little. The word is a name for a compound of qualities producing a complex of results which may have little in common save that they relate to co-work as contrasted with strife in one direction and with isolated work in another. Nor do we know just what the constituents of this compound are. It is not like a chemical compound, always composed of the same elements in the same proportions, but resembles rather a merchant's stock of goods or a banker's portfolio of securities. Of two persons rated as having equal coöperativeness one may have his mainly by virtue of a liking for human companionship, readiness to persuade and be persuaded, tolerance of opposition and conflict, and acceptance of defeat within the organization without rancor; the other may have his mainly by comprehension of the abilities and limitations of himself and his co-workers, readiness to live

[2] Most men of affairs, and some men of science, consider this queer individualistic form of coöperation a weakness in science, and have tried to improve upon it by organizing it in various ways. But it is not certain that they have improved it much.

and let live, the absence of envy, and an unselfish devotion to the enterprise.

What I have said about coöperativeness is true of all the so-called "traits" that refer to human behavior in human relations. Leadership, obedience, courtesy, political ability, executive ability, entrepreneurial ability, or any other such term is a name for a variable congeries of qualities and powers defined mainly by the results it produces. The application is even broader. Almost all the abilities and propensities of man except his sense powers, and perhaps the powers measured by intelligence tests, are compounds undefined or ill-defined as to their constituents and most honestly described by the results they produce.

To return to coöperation as a human relation. It is distinguished from many human relations by the fact that neither party habitually leads in establishing the relation and neither party habitually controls its workings. In theory, at least, the relation is established by a sort of common consent, and controlled by a sort of common recognition and acceptance of the purpose of the coöperative enterprise. Certain exceptions may be taken to this statement, but the contrast is clear between the relation of coöperators and such relations as those of leader and led, ruler and ruled, teacher and taught, mother and child, courter and courted, physician and patient, employer and employee, host and guest, voters and their elected representatives, pastor and flock.

The questions: "Which party instigates the rela-

tion, and how?" and "Which party controls the
relation, and how?" are obviously of importance for
human science and human engineering. They deserve more attention and investigation than they
have received.

In the leader-led relation, the leader by definition
and by fact controls, or the relation vanishes, and he
probably most often establishes the relation also. In
the protector-protected relations, the protector rules,
but the protected commonly establish the relation by
their appeals. The protector may use it to establish a
leader-led or ruler-subject relation. In the ruler-
subject relation the ruler controls, though not absolutely.

From time immemorial until very recently teacher-
taught relations were controlled by the teachers.
Tolstoi and certain apostles of so-called progressive
education have sought to reverse this. In Tolstoi's
school the consequences were disastrous. Of pupil
control in the schools of today you probably know
more than I do. Who instigated the relation a
thousand generations ago when some ancestor of
Tubal Cain taught the young to chip flints, and the
Nimrods of the time taught them the craft of the
hunt, and the old men initiated the young into the
lore and observances of the horde, we do not know.
It is conceivable that all the learners were moved by
what Dewey would call a felt need, and teased the
experts to teach them, but it is to my mind likely that
some of the experts found pleasure in teaching and
sought the pupils out. To "gladly teche" seems to me

as characteristic of human nature as to "gladly
lerne."

The sex relation in courtship and mating has received an enormous amount of attention from poets,
novelists, and entertainers high and low, and some
serious study by medical men, biologists, anthropologists, psychologists, and sociologists. But the exact
roles of man and woman in the establishment and
control of the relation are still not known. The traditional view that man is the prime mover has been
abandoned by modern realistic writers. How far
they did this in the interest of truth and how far in
the interest of entertainment is not for me to decide.
When Bernard Shaw's *Don Juan* shifted the roles of
pursuer and pursued (that was in 1907) it was regarded as an example of his talent for obtaining
surprise and amusement by perversity. Now, only
one generation later, it is the regular thing in attempts
at realistic fiction for the hero to be enticed, pursued,
entrapped, and seduced by almost any means short
of physical violence.

Certain facts in the love-making of man's nearest
relatives, the anthropoid apes, suggest that the fe-
male has a tendency to lure which may precede and
instigate the male's tendency to capture and embrace.
And it seems probable that the caveman extorting
compliance by brute force was less normal than the
caveman smiling, strutting, and showing off his talents, and responding to the coy interest, advances,
and retreats which this behavior evoked in the cave
girl by caressing, pursuit, and capture. Then as now,

probably, the hopeful difficulties which she interposed were potent stimuli to his loverly aggressions.

Each human relation has, in a sense, its special psychology, reporting what original tendencies influence the relation in question, how the individual differences of men in abilities, wants, and propensities influence their behavior in it, and how the experiences and training of persons extend and modify these influences. But I must limit the present discussion to the fundamental psychology of human relations in general.

The first fact to note is the enormous increase in the variety of the situations of life produced by the fact that the same person becomes a score of variants according as he is responded to as your doctor, your friend, your customer, etc., etc. Moreover, the variants produced in the situations Smith, Jones, Brown, etc., when each is responded to as in a certain relation to you, need not all be alike but may vary according to the natures of Smith, Jones, Brown, etc. A simple stereotyped modification will not always suffice. Sometimes it will. A lady who was famed for her success in entertaining clergymen explained her success very simply. "You know," she said, "I always ask them 'What is the greatest compliment you have ever received?' and then the time passes very pleasantly while they report various compliments and discuss the merits of each." Doubtless this would serve well in the hostess-guest relation not only for clergymen but also for many teachers, actors, colonels, psychologists, and others. Similar stereotyped modifications serve more or less well in other relations. The vote-seeker admires the baby of any mother. But in general the situation of person P in relation X is complicated by the varying inter-effects of the relation and person.

A second fact to note is the enormous increase in the variety of the responses of a man to absolutely the same situation produced by the variants in his mental set or adjustment according to the relation in which he finds himself. The same situation will produce the same response in person P only if P is the same in all relevant respects, including such sets of mind as hunger versus satiety, hope versus fear, mastery versus submission, expecting French words versus expecting English words or Spanish words, seeking approval, money, excitement, or peace, thinking of mathematics, religion, politics, or love, being in the relation of father, son, brother, partner, agent, patient, client, or servant.

In the general formula for behavior (situation S evokes response R in person P) person P varies widely according to which of his many mental sets is active, even when the situation is an inanimate object. When it is a human being toward whom person P may stand in a hundred different relations, the variety may be multiplied a hundred fold.

Social behavior or human intercourse is presumably caused in the same way that non-social behavior is, namely by tendencies given by the genes and the circumstances of life operating by repetition and reward, that is by occurrence and reinforcement by the confirming reaction. But the habits are enormously more complicated, so complicated that even scientific thinkers are tempted to invoke magical powers to explain their consequences. And even resolute observers and experimentalists are tempted to stop at wide and vague traits and tendencies instead of pushing on to learn the actual probabilities that elements A, B, C, D, etc., in situations will evoke elements alpha, beta, gamma, delta, etc., in responses.

A third fact of importance is the ability or ease of shifting from one set of mind to another. A man cannot turn his mind as readily as he can turn his eyes, but he can turn it with amazing ease. In law and in logic a human relation is fixed and the legal and logical consequences of being in it are fixed by statutes and definitions. But in reality a person can shift fluently, and even unconsciously, from one relation to another and from one compound of relations to another, and from one treatment of a relation to another. So a mother may at one moment act in the benefactor-benefited relation as by denying herself food to give it to her child and at another in the owner-slave relation as by arraying the child in garments which please her but make it miserable. Few employers stay consistently in the strictly economic treatment of the employer-employee relation, hiring that amount of labor which will maximize their profits, and hiring the most productive workers they can for the amount they have to spend. They may shift to or toward the owner-slave relation, acting as if they had bought the laborer as well as his labor.

They may shift toward the mastery-submission relation, domineering over their employees in unprofitable ways. More happily, they may shift to the protector-protected or benefactor-benefited relation.

This is not to say that the mind easily discards laws and syllogisms when they have been established as customs and conventional doctrines. On the contrary, man is a creature of convention as well as a creature of impulse. And evidence to show man dutifully striving to make his behavior in a given human relation what is fit and proper to that relation is as genuine as evidence of his slippery shifts and illogical mixtures. But in all he is a creature of instincts and habits rather than the reasonably prudent man of law or the lover of consistency of logic. One might indeed argue, though somewhat whimsically, that man's brain is more careless of consistency than his body. His body will not attack and flee, or accept and reject, or swallow and vomit simultaneously, but his mind is able and willing to do almost the equivalents of these inconsistencies, and be A and not A with little if any distress. Certainly the passion of the logician for consistency is one of the rarer human passions.

The genes probably guaranteed early man a fair average degree of competence in perceiving physical objects, avoiding natural perils, obtaining food, producing and rearing offspring, and also in living together profitably in a small tribe or large family group.[3] The genes still account for much of man's

[3] Such a group was the earliest form of the "closed society"

behavior in some human relations, such as those of
courter and courted, husband and wife, mother and
child, member to member in a closed society, protector and protected, leader and led. Indeed, some
of the behavior in these relations may be caused by
genes possessed by many mammals.

But many of the human relations in which the
maintenance, operation, and improvement of civilized life depends are themselves products of a civilized environment, and some of them are among the
most artificial constructions of the environment.
Such are, for example, the relation of parties to a
contract, of lawyer to client, of congressman to his
constituency, and of labor leader to his union on one
hand and to employers on the other, and of the government of one nation to the government of other
nations.

Discovering good or better ways to act in human
relations is a task for all the sciences of man, including history. Good will toward men is not enough.
Moreover, science is needed to inform us how the
specialized and restricted sorts of benevolence which
the genes do provide can develop or be developed
into a general good will. Inventing customs, laws,
and institutions which will favor these good ways of
human intercourse found by science is a task for
politics, legislation, religion, social work, education,

---

in which the relations of man to man were notably different
from the relations of a man in the group to a man outside it.
The outsider was perhaps responded to as a dangerous edible
animal.

and other forms of human engineering. The conjectures of reformers, no matter how well intentioned, are not enough.

These tasks would be hard even if all men belonged to a few fixed types like peas, and were as consistent in their responses as oxygen atoms, and were as logical in their thoughts and motives as Aristotle. They are made harder by the individual differences in men, by the complex action of mental sets with the consequent shifting and combining of relations, by human inconsistencies, and by the frequent dominance of instincts and habits over reasoning, which I have been describing.

It is necessary to face these difficulties. We cannot rest content with an economics that assumes that a hirer of a thousand men at $20 a week receives approximately equal value from each, and talks about entrepreneurial ability as if it were always the same compound of abilities. We cannot rest content with a political science that expects that every individual will be a good, not to say the best, judge of his own interests, and takes it as axiomatic that a person at least knows what he wishes, if not what is to his interest. Or with a science of law that operates with such alleged entities as responsibility or intent, and esteems personal testimony far above circumstantial evidence. It is not right that the human sciences and arts should be built on foundations of false or inadequate psychology. On the other hand, a psychologist would, in my opinion, be utterly foolish to suggest that these edifices be torn down because he does not approve the psychological parts of their foundations. What is required is that the unsafe foundations be replaced by safer ones, and that whatever alterations in the building are necessary be made as far and as soon as they can be made without undue damage to the building as a whole.

As a case interesting in itself as well as useful to test the recommendation just made, we may take the psychology of intent as stated by the leading expert in criminal law of the nineteenth century, Sir James Fitzjames Stephen. Intention, he says,

is the result of deliberation upon motives, and is the object aimed at by the action caused or accompanied by the act of volition. . . .

This account of the nature of intention explains the common maxim which is sometimes stated as if it were a positive rule of law, that a man must be held to intend the natural consequences of his act. I do not think the rule in question is really a rule of law, further or otherwise than as it is a rule of common sense. The only possible way of discovering a man's intention is by looking at what he actually did, and by considering what must have appeared to him at the time the natural consequence of his conduct. . . .

There is, however, a second and more general way in which intention is an element of crime. Intention, as I have already pointed out, is an element of voluntary action, and as all crimes (except crimes of omission) must be voluntary actions, intention is a constituent element of all criminal acts. It would be a mistake to suppose that in order that an act may amount to a crime the offender must intend to commit the crime to which his act amounts, but he must in all cases intend to do the act which constitutes the crime. For instance, there are cases in which a person may commit murder, without intending to commit murder, but no case in which he can commit murder without intending to do the act which makes him a murderer. Suppose, for instance, a robber fires a pistol at the person robbed, intending only to wound him, and does actually kill him, he is guilty of murder, though he had no intention to commit murder, but he cannot be guilty unless he intended to fire the pistol.[4]

There is not a word about the relation in which the person acting stands to the person acted upon; nor about the relations of either of them to the community. The accused is divested of almost everything that a scientific student of crime would be interested in, and left as a deliberator on motives who chooses to perform a certain act, and has knowledge of its natural consequences. The legal man of Stephen is abstract and unreal.

Legal man is, however, perhaps a necessary evil. The law has constructed or selected a psychology that fits its purpose. It is the business of the criminal law to punish certain persons for certain acts forbidden by the law. The person must be responsible in the sense that if anybody is to be punished for the behavior it is he, and in the sense that if the person is legally punishable for any behavior it includes this. In medieval times the law would usually punish a man as surely if it thought that the devil moved him to the deed, as if it thought that the man himself intended it. When it became illegal, so to speak, to punish John Doe for what the devil did in him, the

[4] *A History of the Criminal Law of England*, edition of 1883, II, 110–113, *passim*.

law selected a psychology of responsibility and intention which could be fitted to the customs of the law. The customs of the law are the deciding factor. Justice Cardozo opposed an argument from modern psychology by saying, "To hold that motive or temptation is equivalent to coercion is to plunge the law into endless difficulties."

This is defensible, and probably advisable, and I repeat that psychology should proceed cautiously and modestly in its criticisms and recommendations to law, government, economics, business, education, philanthropic work, and other sciences and arts of men, lest it "plunge them into endless difficulties." But is it not also fair to ask that these sciences and arts should promptly learn and use the relevant facts in the science of psychology lest in their fear of endless difficulties they fail to outgrow dangerous simplifications and fantasies?

## IV

# THE PSYCHOLOGY OF LANGUAGE

Language is man's greatest invention. It is a social tool more important than the community, the state, the law, the church, or the school. It is an intellectual tool as important as observation and experiment, and more important than logic. It is more important than all the physical tools invented in the last two thousand years. These assertions may well seem extravagant, but they can be justified. At all events the psychology of language is important enough to deserve your attention for two of our meetings.

Let us consider first the function of language. It is commonly said that the function of language, the service it performs in satisfying human wants, is to express thoughts or feelings. This statement is inadequate. Language is used not only to express but also to arouse thoughts and feelings and still more to arouse movements. The relation of most importance is not the parallelism between the words and the inner life of the one who uses them but the effect upon the one who hears or sees them. The function of language is fundamentally just the same as that of pushing, pulling, paying money to, feeding, clothing, knocking down, or helping up an animal. It is to produce responses on the animal's part, to get him to think or feel or do something. We do not talk exclusively for the sake of expressing our mental condition any more than we pay men money exclusively to express our satisfaction with their services.

It may be objected that I have misunderstood "express" as meaning some mere outpouring like the shriek of pain or the sob of grief, that in the present case it really means "communicate," and that the function of language *is* to communicate thoughts and feelings.

The statement so amended is still inadequate. For action by the one spoken to is not covered by it. When we say "Shut the door" or "If you wait, you shall have a dime" our aim is not to communicate our desire or intention but to secure certain behavior. What we really do communicate is not at all our own state of mind, our desire or intention, nor is there any reason why we should. Of course in the strict sense we could not communicate it if we would; we cannot pass on our inner states as they are. If anything is communicated, if the boy thinks about our thoughts at all, he would think, not "*I* want the door shut" but "*He* wants the door shut," not "*I'll* give him a dime if *he* waits" but "*He* intends to give *me* a dime if *I* wait." Moreover, in the case of almost every declaratory sentence what is "communicated" is not the speaker's own mental state. For instance, I say, "I feel cold and hungry and sleepy." "John was very angry with me yesterday." "It is raining." In the first case I speak not to make you cold or hungry or sleepy but to arouse sympathy or pardon. In the

second, I speak not to duplicate in you my memory
or even to inform you about it, but to inform you
about John's feeling or behavior. In the third case
similarly I wish you to be aware, not that a certain
perception is occurring in me, but that a certain
event is occurring in nature.

All this is perhaps too obvious to be mentioned,
but I very much fear that devotion to the egocentric
theory of language would have led some of you to
evade the countless cases of disparity between the
mental state causing a speech and the mental state
resulting in the person spoken to if concrete cases of
it were not given.

Indeed, it is to be feared that the devotees of that
theory will attempt a further evasion and argue that,
even supposing the ultimate function of language to
be the production of responses of any sort, of thought
or of feeling or of action, bearing no necessary like-
ness to the state of the speaker, still the proximate
function of language is to express or communicate
thoughts and feelings, the final response of the hearer
being always mediated by his appreciation of the
speaker's state of mind. But it is necessary not only
to admit that in the end language serves to modify
the hearer, and in all sorts of ways, but also to admit
that the modification in him may in certain cases
come without any paralleling by him of the speaker's
thought or of any part or feature of it whatsoever.
Honest consideration of any hundred random cases
of the use of language will abundantly prove this.
When the two-year-old child comes, opens his mouth,

or holds up his hands in response to his nurse's "Come
here," "Open your mouth," "Pat-a-cake," etc., it is
certainly incredible that he thinks "Nurse wants me
to come" or "Nurse wants me to open my mouth" or
"Nurse wants me to hold up my hands." Nor indeed
does an adult go through such a fruitless psychological analysis of the mind of, say, a physician who asks
him to come, open his mouth, put out his tongue, etc.
Who can maintain that at every meal every "Pass the
bread," "Did you have a good sleep?" "Do you like
bacon and eggs?" and the like is echoed in one's mind
by "She wants me to pass the bread," "She wonders if
I had a good sleep," "He wants to know whether I
like bacon and eggs," etc.? Honest observation forces
one to see that in most cases he responds to a servant's
"Come this way, please" directly with no awareness
of her thought or anybody's thought.

Although the general function of language is to
arouse feelings and acts as well as thoughts in the
hearer, the arousal of thoughts is its special function
and its most important work. And although the
thought aroused in the hearer need not duplicate the
thought that caused the speaker to say what he did,
there is often resemblance between the two, sometimes almost complete resemblance. In declarative
sentences expressing facts of nature or fancies of the
imagination external to both speaker and hearer, such
as "John came yesterday"; "The cow is in the barn";
"It looks like rain"; "Two and two make four"; "The
moon is the daughter of the sun," resemblance is the
rule. A single word spoken with no aura of question,

command, emotion, or accessory ideas also commonly arouses much the same meaning in the hearer that it had for the speaker. As I say and you hear the words red, green, four, six, Boston, Cambridge, Plato, Darwin, fairy, centaur, we all have pretty much the same facts and fancies in mind.

Words, phrases, and sentences used thus impersonally to arouse their customary meanings in the hearer's mind are language par excellence. They can be the common possession of the tribe, stored in memory, and listed and described in dictionaries. They are the invention in its fully developed form, a tool whereby a man can arouse in others ideas which have been aroused in him or sprung up in him from the inner workings of his own brain.

By simple and straightforward extensions every person that is born receives a name that means him; every island, mountain, river, and species of animal or plant that is discovered receives a name that means it; every happening to every one of billions of persons, animals, chairs, balls, cakes, pies, stars, storms, etc., etc., may receive a sentence that records it. Every quality or condition of size, shape, color, tone, etc., and every potency in action that man discerns he is likely to name.

The invention of written language not only enables man to store facts and fancies otherwise than in the memories of persons and to speak to men unseen or even unborn, but also reacts upon spoken language. Subtle and complicated things, qualities, events, and relations which a man could not organize and express in speech even to himself, may be wrought into paragraphs and books by written composition with consultation at any point of all that he has written so far. Linguistic procedures devised for and familiarized by writing and reading may later be used in speech.

By subtler elaborations the facts and relations discovered by chemists lead to the language or symbolism of chemistry, which relates the characters, affinities, and adventures of ninety-odd heroes named H, O, C, N, etc., making legions of exactly described substances from $H_2O$ and $CO_2$ to $p$-$NH_2$ $C_6$ $H_4$ $SO_2$ $NH_2$ and other drugs that cure us, dyes that adorn us, and hormones that manage our lives.

The facts and relations discovered by mathematicians lead to the languages or symbolisms of arithmetic, algebra, calculus, and geometry from the simple series 1, 2, 3, 4, 5, etc., to $n!$, $\sqrt{-1}$, $\int_0^\infty$, $\overrightarrow{AB}$, and from imaginaries, differentials, integrals, and vectors on to terms about space of $n$ dimensions and quantum theory.

These are well-nigh perfect languages, of great scope and power, free from ambiguities, but essentially as simple as expressing 8 by holding up all the fingers of one hand and three fingers of the other. Think of a few of these linguistic triumphs, such as the decimal series from .000,000,001 or less to 999,-999,999 or more, filled with additive steps as small as you please. Think of the language of exponents, positive, negative, and fractional, whereby, for example, the curves (segments of which are shown on the opposite page) relating the magnitude of $y$ to the magnitude of $x$ are perfectly described by the equations $y = x^{1.5}$, $y = x^{1.333}$, $y = x^{1.25}$, $y = x^{1.167}$, $y = x$, $y = x^{0.75}$, and $y = x^{0.5}$.

Think of the equations of physics — the most pregnant sentences ever said or written about the physical world.

If and when the social sciences become able to describe and predict the behavior of man somewhat as physics and chemistry can now describe and predict the behavior of matter, they too will have their language of words and other symbols representing psychological and social forces and relations.

The variety and complexity of language are almost beyond belief. The number of different commands or requests that were given by persons in this country during the past week was probably far above a billion. The number of different questions asked during the week was probably even larger. The number of different statements made was surely above a million million. The New Yorker pokes fun at writers whom it finds using the same descriptive phrase half a dozen times in a hundred-thousand-word book. And we are amused by its quotations, for example by the lizards and old marble in the following excerpts:

Under her shining black hair there peeped out a small, delicate, lizard-like face, of the mellow tint of fine old marble. — Page 82.

Under their lace, her slim well-poised neck and her bosom and shoulders gleamed with the mellow softness of fine old marble. — Page 88.

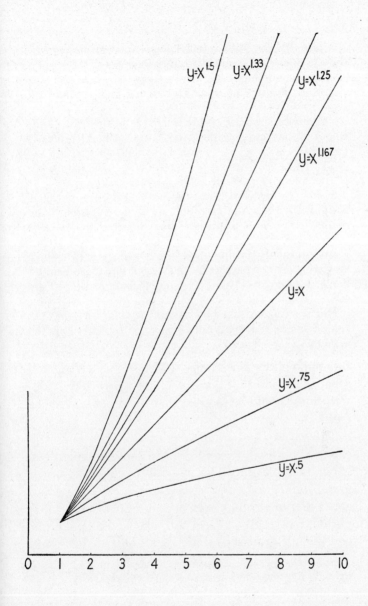

Marie Auguste, her small delicate face gleaming with the radiance of fine old marble. — Page 95.

. . . she contemplated her body which was soft and slim and of the colour of an old and noble marble. — Page 104.

Affectedly she carried her small delicate head of the colour of fine old marble through the brilliant rooms. — Page 145.

The Duke . . . struck her on the . . . face, which was of the colour of ancient, noble marble. — Page 239.

So she sat on Christmas Eve, frail and delicate, all in white foamy lace, out of which, of the hue of an old and noble marble, the lizard-like face flickered maliciously. — Page 267.

And suddenly turning upon him her elegant, lizard-like face which shone palely like an old and fine marble under her gleaming black hair, she smiled maliciously. — Page 403.

Her small lizard-like head, with the clear forehead the colour of fine old marble, looked delicate and desirable. — Page 452.[1]

But the wonder is that any writer should avoid such repetitions, and that our expectancy of variety in descriptions should be so great that the repetition seems inept.

The variety and complexity of what our language can say is literally infinite in the sense of countless. If one is free to speak not only of green grass, brown grass, long grass, short grass, soft grass, stiff grass, and other realizable grasses but also of red, blue, purple, red-green, particolored, checkered, and other conceivable grasses, and to say not only that the said

[1] *The New Yorker*, December 13, 1941, p. 452. Copyrighted. Reprinted by permission of *The New Yorker*.

grass grows, dies, appears, lies, is eaten, nourishes, and acts in other reasonable ways, but also that it nods, beckons, whispers, laughs, cries, mourns, remembers, loves, and performs other fanciful or absurd acts, and to say not only that it does such quickly, slowly, often, always, rarely, once in ten times, once in a hundred times but also that it does such lovingly, gladly, regretfully, ambitiously, wisely, unwisely, and in other ways that a poet, insane man, or lexicographer might think of, we can easily make a billion sentences about some kind of grass doing something somehow, no two of which say or mean the same. Let us use phrases of locality like "on Boston Common" or "in the Garden of Eden," and we can easily add five more ciphers to the 1,000,000,000. Let us use a temporal or conditional clause and we can add five more. Let us also tack on a conclusion or reflection sanely or unsanely suggested by the given fact or fancy about the grass and we shall have more different statements about grass than there are blades of grass in the world.

Each of these billions of little speeches about grass can have meaning for us when we say it and for any qualified person who hears it. And in general, in statements or declarative sentences, the speaker's words mean something to him. If the hearer understands or misunderstands the words they mean something to him. The speaker intends the words to mean something to the hearers, or, more exactly, to the persons spoken to. The words are used by the speaker as signs or symbols. They are symbols of individual things, persons, and events, of groups or classes of things, persons, or events, or of any member of a certain group or class. They can also be symbols of abstract qualities (such as sourness, length, weight, desirability, or impossibility) that are isolable in thought but not in fact, and of relations and groups of relations between things, events, and qualities. A "speech," that is a word or series of words operating in the speaker-hearer relation, can, in fact, mean anything that anybody can think of.

All this is true and more or less useful to bear in mind, but it is explaining the fact of meaning by itself. Can we get to a deeper level or broader survey that can tell us more about meaning than it itself tells?

From 1920 to 1922 in various periodicals, and in 1923 in the book *The Meaning of Meaning*, Ogden and Richards discussed verbal symbols and their meanings with great cleverness and subtlety. Those of you who have never read this book can do so with interest and profit. To those who wish a short and simple account of the main facts about meaning to compare with that which I shall give, I commend the chapter on Meaning (Chapter 9) of Bloomfield's *Language*, and pages 63 to 80 of Eisenson's *Psychology of Speech*.

The essential fact of meaning to the hearer revealed by Ogden and Richards' book and by the various descriptions and explanations of meaning by psychologists and experts in linguistic theory seems to me to be the very simple fact that the meaning of an ordinary declarative sentence to the hearer is what it makes him think or think of, or tend to think or think of, or avoid thinking or thinking of, or tend to avoid thinking or thinking of.

The older accounts of the meaning of words to hearers dwelt too exclusively upon their power to make him think of objects, and to think of them in the form of memory images. The older scheme of the mind's contents and its operations in having, or being aware of, meanings is as shown below.

| *In Experience* | *In Understanding* |
|---|---|
| Word connects with object, e.g., *Rover* connects with a particular dog. | Word evokes an image, e.g., *Rover* evokes an image of that particular dog. |
| *dog* connects with black dog<br>" " white dog<br>" " small dog<br>" " large dog<br>" " etc. | *dog* evokes a series of images, or a collection of nascent images, or a generalized schematic image. |

The evocation of images is only a small part of what happens when a person thinks the meaning of a word or sentence. A person's past experiences in connection with a heard word or sentence have been far more than a string of perceived objects, and all of his past experiences can be influential in determining what he thinks when he hears it the next time. A word naming a thing means what the thing has done as truly as what it looks, or sounds, or feels like. The pleasure or pain received from the thing are potent determiners of the word's meaning, but rarely appear in imagery. Any responses of action or feeling ever connected to the word by a hearer can and do influence its future meaning. *Father* is not only such a size and shape, but also a "to run to," a "to kiss," and a "to ask permission of." As fast as words enter our experience, each of them tends to evoke the sounds and meanings of *other words* that have gone with it, especially those whose connections with it have been OK'd by the confirming reaction. Many words, like *is, have, and, but,* and *to,* refer to relations which, in most minds, have no imaginal parallels, counterparts, or affiliates whatsoever. Many pairs of meanings are of pairs of facts which never have been distinguished in perception or imagery, such as 284 chickens and 285 chickens, or lights of wave lengths 6438 or 6439 Angströms, or sounds of 7.82 and 7.83 decibels, or angles of 29° 20′ and 29° 21′.

What will any given word or series of words make the hearer think or think of? Here again the general answer is fairly simple. It will make him think the thoughts that have been connected with it in his past experience, especially those whose connections with it have been accompanied or closely followed by resultant satisfaction to himself; and it will make him think *of* the sights, sounds, wishes, hopes, fears, runnings, graspings, and other experiences of perception, emotion, or action that have been connected with it in his past experiences, especially those whose connections with it have satisfied him.

Experience operates by the forces of occurrence and after-effects, repetition and reinforcement by the confirming reaction, no less in forming connections between words heard and the thoughts which they evoke than it does in forming simpler and more obvious connections.

In the case of a word that means one particular concrete person or thing, such as the hearer's father, the word father has often accompanied or closely preceded or followed the sight (smell, and touch) of that person; and if, when heard in his absence, it calls up an expectation of him, the after-effects are more satisfying than if it calls up some other expectation or none. For example, the child who hears "See Father," or "Here comes Father," and has an expectation of him before he turns and sees him is surely better satisfied than if he had had an expectation of "Doggie" or "Nursie" or "Bottle." In the latter case there would have been a frustration or disappointment of the child's expectation and no confirming reaction would have been issued to strengthen the connection. Whether he is better satisfied than if he had had none is somewhat less certain, but there is evidence to show that the fulfillment of an expectation is, other things being equal, satisfying. The child who hears "Go kiss Father" or "Give the ball to Father" and has an expectation or image or reference to Father rather than to Doggie or Nursie which directs his behavior will probably receive satisfying praise and petting.

Later in the child's life songs and stories are satisfying in proportion as the words evoke the right meanings rather than the wrong or none.

How the forces of occurrence and after-effect make

a person think of the appropriate event when he hears "Doggie barks," and of the appropriate relations when he hears "on," "in," and "under," and of the appropriate qualities or features when he hears "hot," "cold," "long," "short," "two," and "three," and of the appropriate classes of things or qualities or events or relations when he hears "a dog," "a color," "a running," "a similarity," and the like, I will not now describe, but I could show that the role of after-effects and the confirming reaction is important in all these cases.

If we took the time to present the evidence, you would, I think, accept repetition and reward (i.e., reinforcement by the confirming reaction) as the causes of all such attachments of meanings. They are really just extensions of such cases as the following: Hearing *rōt* makes an Englishman think of a certain act and a German think of a certain color, because of the experiences connected with *wrote* and *roth*. Hearing *sīn* makes many mathematicians think of a certain trigonometrical ratio, many philologists think of symbol, and many stenographers think of writing one's name by hand, because the respective connections have been frequent and satisfactory to the respective persons. We think what we do when we hear *tü, fōr, siks, ten* in certain contexts because these arithmetical meanings were repeated and rewarded in our schooling.

The strengthening of mental connections by repetition and reward accounts for the meanings of single words and common phrases. Can these forces ac-

count also for the meanings of new and often complicated combinations of words and sentences? Let
us take a moment for an illustration. You all will get
meanings, and substantially identical meanings, from
this sentence never before heard. "If a psychologist
should propose to high officers in the United States
army that some of the most gifted young soldiers be
made assistants to colonels and generals, with the
expectation that some of them might soon be promoted to be colonels or generals, he could support
his proposal by facts concerning the importance of
native ability as compared with general experience,
and by facts concerning the importance of special
training as compared with general training." It
should be admitted at once that the systems of mental connections that are adequate to give a hearer
the meanings of familiar words and of series of words
in familiar patterns like "if a psychologist," or "in the
United States army," or "assistants to colonels and
generals," are not adequate to deal similarly with
novel concatenations and interrelations of such patterns in such a complex sentence as our sample.

Consider the results when 200 pupils in grade six
are given the following sentence and asked the following questions about it: [2]

In Franklin, attendance upon school is required of
every child between the ages of seven and fourteen on
every day when school is in session unless the child is so

[2] The sentence and questions were presented in print, and
each child could read them as often as he wished, and as carefully.

ill as to be unable to go to school, or some person in his house is ill with a contagious disease, or the roads are impassable.

1. What is the general topic of the paragraph?
2. On what day would a ten-year-old girl not be expected to attend school?
3. Between what years is attendance upon school compulsory in Franklin?
4. How many causes are stated which make absence excusable?

### Answers to Question 1

Unanswered
Franklin
In Franklin
Franklin attendance
Franklin School
Franklin attending school
Days of Franklin
School days of Franklin
Doings at Franklin
Pupils in Franklin
Franklin attends to his school
It is about a boy going to Franklin
It was a great inventor
Because its a great invention
The attendance of the children
The attendance in Franklin
School
To tell about school
About school
What the school did when the boy was ill
What the child should take
If the child is ill
How old a child should be
If the child is sick or contagious disease

Illness
On diseases
Very ill
An cxcusc
The roads are impassable
Even rods are impossible
A few sentences
Made of complete sentences
A sentence that made sense
A group of sentences making sense
A group of sentences
Subject and predicate
Subject
The sentence
A letter
Capital
A capital letter
To begin with a capital
The first word
A general topic
Good topic
Leave half an inch space
The heading
Period
An inch and a half
An inch and a half capital letter
The topic is civics
The answer

Most of these children knew the meanings of the words in this paragraph and this question. As you have noted, few of the errors trace back to having wrong meanings or none for single words. Their errors are in the main caused by errors in maneuvering their mental connections, not in having wrong or useless ones.

ne years ago I had large numbers of children
many paragraphs new to them, made up of
r easy words but rather complexly organized.
ᴛʜᴇ variety of errors was in all cases comparable
to those of the sixth-grade children with the question about the rule for school attendance. At first
, sight, they baffled explanation. But an explanation
was found in the shape of two principles that
tell not only how those who made the errors went
wrong, but also how those who made no errors went
right.

The first is the principle of potencies or weights.
To get the right meaning of a total, the meaning of
each element must be given the right potency or
weight in comparison with the others. Consider the
influence of overpotency of the word paragraph in
the question "What is the general topic of the paragraph?" This causes or helps to cause such errors as:
*A sentence that made sense, A group of sentences
making sense, A group of sentences, A few sentences.*
When the *t o p* of topic is overpotent also we have
such responses as: *Leave half an inch space, The
heading, An inch and a half, An inch and a half capital letter,* and (from another group) *The topic of
paragraph is one inch in.*

Consider overpotency of elements of the paragraph itself, beginning with the word Franklin. This
caused or helped to cause the responses *Franklin, In
Franklin, Franklin attending school, Days of Franklin, School days of Franklin, Franklin attends to his
school,* and *It is about a boy going to Franklin.* Still

stronger evidence is given by *It was a great inventor* and *Because it's a great invention*. If you inspect the responses of five hundred children in grades 5 to 8 you will find abundant evidence of the influence of overpotency in the fact that to any of the questions about the paragraph some child is likely to have his answer determined by Franklin with little weight attached to anything else in the paragraph or the question. For example: On what day would a ten-year-old girl not be expected to attend school? Answer: Franklin. Between what years is attendance upon school compulsory in Franklin? Answer: Franklin was in school 141 years.

Even a rather unimpressive word like seven may be given so much weight as to distort comprehension and produce: What is the general topic of the paragraph? Answer: Seven and fourteen; Answer: How old a child should be. Between what years is attendance compulsory in Franklin? Answer: Seven years. How many causes are stated which make absence excusable? Answer: Under seven.

Similar evidence appeared in my five hundred records for the words *attendance, school, every, ill, contagious, disease,* and *impassable*. We have answers for the four questions as follows:

### Questions

1. What is the general topic of the paragraph?
2. On what day would a ten-year-old girl not be expected to attend school?
3. Between what years is attendance upon school compulsory in Franklin?

4. How many causes are stated which make absence excusable?

*Answers*

(testifying to the overpotency of *attendance, school, every,* etc.)

attendance    1. Attendance.
2. To attendance with Franklin.
3. In Franklin attendance upon school is required. 3. Attending school 130 days.

school    1. School. 1. They must know their lessons.
2. In the beginning of school.
3. School in session. 3. In the years of school.

every    1. Every child.
2. Expected every day. 2. On every day.
3. Every year. 3. Every child between fourteen or thirteen.
4. Every day.

ill    1. Illness. 1. Very ill. 1. If the child is ill.
2. Ill. 2. A very bad throat.
3. He cannot go to school unless ill.
4. When child is ill. 4. Must be sick.

contagious    1. Contagious disease.
2. If she is sick or has a contagious disease.
3. Contagious disease.
4. Contagious disease.

disease    1. Fever. 1. About disease.
2. Often sick.
3. Unless ill or contagious disease. 3. Disease.
4. A terrible disease going out. 4. Because when a boy has disease.

impassable    1. The roads are impassable. 1. Snow.
2. When roads are impassable.

    3. Seven to fourteen years or the roads are
       impassable.
    4. Or the roads are impassable.

This principle of potencies or weights is so important that I shall give you one more illustration to remember it by.

One of the paragraphs read:

You need a coal range in winter for kitchen warmth and for continuous hot-water supply, but in summer, when you want a cool kitchen and less hot water, a gas range is better. The *xyz* ovens are safe. In the end ovens there is an extra set of burners for broiling.

The *x y z* was used instead of the advertiser's name to avoid propaganda for any private business, no matter how deserving. Now I dare to predict that no matter what question you ask about the paragraph, some pupil in grade 5 or 6 will be misled by over-potency of even this barren sequence of letters. With a few hundred children I got the following:

What two varieties of stoves does the paragraph mention?
"*xyz*." "Gas range and *xyz*."
"*xyz* ovens and end ovens."

What is needed to provide a supply of hot water all day long?
"The *xyz* ovens are safe."

For what purpose is the extra set of burners?
"The *xyz* ovens."

In what part of the stove are they situated?
"The *xyz* oven side."

The influence of underpotency could be shown as clearly, from the responses to questions about various paragraphs, but I will only give one illustration. The paragraph being:

It may seem at first thought that every boy and girl who goes to school ought to do all the work that the teacher wishes done. But sometimes other duties prevent even the best boy or girl from doing so. If a boy's or girl's father died and he had to work afternoons and evenings to earn money to help his mother, such might be the case. A good girl might let her lessons go undone in order to help her mother by taking care of the baby

and the question being

What are some conditions that might make even the best boy leave school work unfinished?

we find as a result chiefly of underpotency of "Even the best boy" the following: *Play, Go playing in the streets, To play ball, Bad, Idleness, Conduct, misbehavior, inattention.*

Getting the right meaning of a complex and novel paragraph or sentence implies not only using all of its elements in coöperation, but also giving each of them its proper weight.

Whatever power in you enabled you to understand the sentence about the psychologist, be it a Wundtian apperception, or an old-fashioned reasoning soul, or, as I believe, an over-all organization of connections and readinesses to connect, did so largely by giving each element a reasonable provisional weight as word after word was heard, and varying these weights if desirable to make a reasonable whole, as the sentence progressed further and as it ended.

The second principle which appears from the study of mistakes in meaning is that the elements must be put and kept in the right relations. In practice, in European languages, this is largely a matter of giving the right meanings to inflectional endings. word order, conjunctions, prepositions, and pronouns, in each case with due regard to the provisional meaning of the sentence as it progresses. All competent students of linguistic or of psychological science will vouch for this second principle, and I need say no more about it.

You will remember that this long excursion into the problem of getting the meaning of complex and novel sentences was undertaken in relation to the question "Can all meanings in a hearer's mind be accounted for by two facts: (1) the connections which words and series of words have made in a person's experience and (2) the reinforcement which these connections received from the confirming reaction?" It appears, at least to me, that if these connections can build themselves into an over-all organization, the answer is *yes*.

## V

## THE PSYCHOLOGY OF LANGUAGE (CONTINUED):
## THE ORIGIN OF LANGUAGE

NOBODY KNOWS when, where or how speech originated, and I am stepping in where wise scholars in linguistics and psychology fear to tread. My theory of the matter is frankly speculative, but I hope that it will be instructive. My colleagues in psychology will, I beg, permit this divagation into speculation by one who has labored long in the less exciting fields of experiment and statistics. I ask and expect no mercy from experts in linguistic science, but only that they build a better theory on the ruins they make of mine.

We must first glance at three time-honored and then dishonored theories, now known by these opprobrious names: ding-dong theory, bow-wow theory, and pooh-pooh theory.

The ding-dong theory assumed a mystical power of certain things to evoke certain sounds from men. Since each such sound was associated with the experience of the thing, it came to mean it. And since men were alike in their responses to things by sounds, one of these sounds meant more or less the same thing to all in the group, and easily became a vehicle of communication. All the evidence is against the existence of any such mystical power, and only extremely strong evidence would induce any scientific student of psychology or of language to put any faith in so extremely unlikely an origin of language.

The bow-wow theory supposed that men formed habits of using the sounds made by animals, things, or events to mean the respective animals, things, and events, and that these habits started them on the road to inventing other sounds as signs of animals, things, or events. For various reasons this theory is discredited. Doubtless after man has language he will often make the sounds that animals and things make, but it is doubtful how often he will do so in a languageless group. Possibly he will do so only accidentally as a part of his general vocal play. There might be little agreement in the ideas evoked in the members of a human group by hearing the varying sounds which its various members made when they thought of a dog, a cow, thunder, and the like.

Even if a group got a sufficient agreement in the case of forty or fifty sounds for these to be used commonly in the group, an advance by the addition of non-mimetic sounds as signs of things and events would be difficult. If the mimetic sounds remained fully mimetic, it might well be impossible. But the opponents of the bow-wow theory have not considered sufficiently the possibility that a human group might modify their vocabulary of mimetic sounds by slurring, abbreviation, and other processes that make speech easier for the speaker without losing the old meanings of animals, things, and events in the hearer. If close imitations of a dog's barking, cock's crowing, baby's crying, lamb's bleating, etc., became conventionalized within a human group into sounds no more like the originals than *bow-wow, cocka-doodle-doo, mama,* and *bah-bah,* or *urr-urr, uk-a-duk-a-duk-duk, na-na,* and *buh-buh,* that group could in a few generations progress to a set of sounds many of which would mean primarily certain animals or things and only secondarily or not at all the sound made by the respective animals and things. The group's vocabulary would all be about things that had distinctive sounds, but could be in the form of sounds different from these and in some cases hardly suggestive of them. The invention of a non-mimetic sound for something hitherto nameless would then be easier. The use of such an invention would, of course, spread somewhat slowly within the group and very slowly outside it to groups accustomed only to mimetic words.

The pooh-pooh theory, or interjectional theory, supposed that the instinctive unlearned cries of man as a wordless animal, which already are sounds that are evoked by certain situations and evoke in human hearers certain equally unlearned responses of action and feeling, came to possess meanings also, and that on the basis of this vocabulary of familiar sounds meaning pain, surprise, fear, affection, and the like, early man here and there used other sounds to mean other facts.

Nobody should doubt that part of this is true. To a mother whose baby cries and seeks her breast that cry probably *means* that the baby wants to be fed if anything means anything to her. If she can think of anything she will think of that, as well as react appropriately to it. But for various reasons students of language have decided that the attachment of meanings to the hearing or the making of these sounds of instinctive nature is not adequate to originate articulate speech. So-called animal language plus the power of thinking meanings would not produce human language.

An ingenious theory has been set forth by Sir Richard Paget, a physicist and student of phonetics, who argues that the total behavior of a man to a situation includes characteristic movements of the tongue and lips and other organs of speech. These gestures of the mouth parts became specially important when a man's hands were "in continual use . . . for craftsmanship, the chase, and the beginnings of art and literature," so that he could not gesture with them. Sounds were added to these "mouthings," and finally came to play the leading role. In Paget's own words:

Originally man expressed his ideas by gesture, but as he gesticulated with his hands, his tongue, lips and jaw unconsciously followed suit in a ridiculous fashion, "understudying" (as Sir Henry Hadow aptly suggested to me) the action of the hands. The consequence was that when, owing to pressure of other business, the principal actors (the hands) retired from the stage — as much as principal actors ever do — their understudies — the tongue, lips and jaw — were already proficient in the pantomimic art.

Then the great discovery was made that if while making a gesture with the tongue and lips, air was blown through the oral or nasal cavities, the gesture became audible as a whispered speech sound. If, while pantomiming with tongue, lips and jaw our ancestors sang, roared or grunted — in order to draw attention to what they were doing — a still louder and more remarkable effect was produced, namely, what we call voiced speech. . . .

In this way there was developed a new system of conventional gesture of the organs of articulation from which, as I suggest, nearly all human speech took its origin. . . .

We can now form a mental picture of how the process of speech-making actually began, but an example or two will make the argument clearer. If the mouth, tongue and lips be moved as in eating, this constitutes a gesture sign meaning "eat"; if, while making this sign, we blow air through the vocal cavities, we automatically produce the whispered sounds mnyΔm-mnyΔm (mnyum), or mnɪΔ-mnɪΔ (mnyuh) — words which probably would be almost universally understood, and which actually occur as a children's word for food in Russian, as well as in English. . . .

Another adult example may be given, namely, in connection with the beckoning gesture — commonly made by extending the hand, palm up, drawing it inwards towards the face and at the same time bending the fingers inwards towards the palm. This gesture may be imitated with the tongue, by protruding, withdrawing, and bending up its tip as it re-enters the mouth and falls to rest.

If this "gesture" be blown or voiced, we get a resultant whispered or phonated *word*, like ʃдə, ʃðə or ʃðva (according to the degree of contact between tongue and upper lip or palate) suggestive of the Icelandic hʃðv, the Hindustani idhar and the Slavonic ɪdʃɪ — all of which bear much the same meaning as our English word "hither." If the same tongue gesture be finished more vigorously, the resultant word will end in a *k* or *g*, owing to the back portion of the tongue making a closure against the soft palate.

Thus, by unconsciously using the tongue, lips, jaw, etc., in the place of the head, hands, etc., pantomimic gesture would almost automatically produce human speech.[1]

Paget fabricated words by moving his own jaws, tongue, and lips in ways which seemed to him likely to have been used as oral gestures of primitive men accompanying manual or other gestures meaning reach up, draw back suddenly, scrape, wave aloft, shoot with a bow and arrow, sew, blow, plough, strip grains from the stalk, pick berries, collect them, and bury them in the ground, and many others. He finds substantial correspondences between his fabricated sounds and certain words in old languages. Of the famous Aryan roots he considers that 77 per cent are clearly pantomimic. For example, "tank – contract, compress – as in thong, is due to two compressions in succession fore and aft the palate"; "da – give – seems to be an offering gesture made with the tongue."[2]

Paget's book (*Human Speech*) is so recent (1930) that his theory has not yet received a pet name. Using the first illustration that he gives we might call

---

[1] R. Paget, *Human Speech* (1930), pp. 133–138, *passim.* Quoted by permission of the publishers, Harcourt, Brace and Company, New York.

[2] *Ibid.*, p. 149. Quoted by permission of the publishers, Harcourt, Brace and Company.

it the yum-yum theory. This, however, really misrepresents and unduly favors it; for the theory requires the mouth parts to pantomime not eating, drinking, sipping, blowing, and other acts of the mouth parts themselves (nobody doubts that), but movements of other parts of the body. A truer nickname would be the "tongue-tied" theory, meaning that the tongue is yoked with the body by subtle bonds of mimetic kinship. The theory has been accepted by at least one psychologist, Eisenson, but it has not been acceptable generally. Personally, I do not believe that any human being before Sir Richard Paget ever made any considerable number of gestures with his mouth parts in sympathetic pantomime with gestures of his hands, arms, and legs, still less that any considerable number of men in any local community made the same oral gestures in such pantomime.

And now for my theory, which is a humdrum affair compared with any of these four.

Let us assume a group of one or more human families living together at least as continuously as one of the groups of chimpanzees studied by Nissen in their natural habitat. Let us assume that their environment includes, besides the untouched objects of nature, a few objects chosen and preserved as tools — say a few pounders, a few cutters, a few gourds, shells, or other dippers and holders, and perhaps a few stabbers and scrapers; and also some natural objects chosen and preserved as playthings, things that one can chew on, roll or throw, make a noise with, and the like.

We may safely assume further that these humans made a wide variety of movements with their hands, much the same as the human infants of today instinctively make, pushing, pulling, tearing, putting into their mouths, dropping out therefrom, dropping, throwing, picking up, etc., etc.

We may safely assume further that these humans made a variety of sounds like the meaningless prattle of infants, letting their mouth parts play with their voices in the same multifarious way that their hands play with any obtainable object. The variety of sounds made may indeed have been greater than that made by an infant of today, whose vocal play may be narrowed by the elimination of sounds which are alien to the language which his environment favors. And we know that an infant of today makes a much wider variety of articulate sounds than the language of his parents contains.

Such a person in such a group would at an early age have a memory image, or expectation, or idea, of the appearance of the person who nursed him which her voice or smell or caress could evoke though she was unseen. By having been experienced in so many different contexts, some image or expectation or idea referring to her would have acquired an existence independent of any particular sequence of behavior. In a similar manner he would have an image or expectation or idea referring to each object that had been associated with many varying concomitants in his uses of it or play with it.

Such a person would prattle while he worked or played much as a child of a year or two now prattles

plays. If his making a certain sound became
:ted with his experiencing a certain object or
d having an image or expectation or idea of
ject or act, he would have a language. That
sound and the act of making it would mean that
object or act to him. It would be a private language,
useless as yet for communication. It would be a narrow language, consisting of only a few words referring mostly to his own acts and possessions, to the
persons in the family group, and to their acts and
posesssions. But it would be genuine language.

And it would be a valuable intellectual tool for its
possessor, enabling him to replace the somewhat
cumbrous and elusive images or expectations by
sounds that he could make and arrange more or less
at will. If he did connect *ik* with his digging stick,
and *üg* with his large turtle-shell container, *yum* with
truffle, and *kuz* with clam, he could plan an expectation to get truffles or one to get clams more easily and
conveniently than he could with only pictorial memories. Consequently, we may safely reckon that
any person who made these connections that gave
sounds meanings and gave things symbolic equivalents would keep them, even though he alone understood them.

What now is the probability that a person brought
up in a languageless family group would form one
such connection whereby a sound (not an instinctive
cry of pain, delight, triumph, etc.) meant an object?
What is the probability that he would form two
such? Three? Four? A dozen? A score?

Properly planned experiments with enough infants brought up in a languageless environment for ten years (perhaps for a much shorter time) would give a decisive answer. I have long wished to make systematic observations of infants in linguistically poor, i.e., underprivileged, environments, but have never been able to find the time, and must rely upon memories of casual observations of my children and grandchildren in making my estimates.

I think that the probability that a person in the top half of the species for intelligence by birth would make four or five such connections is very high, at least seven out of ten. Consider a child of early man playing with a large shell used as a container in the household and prattling as he plays. Let us take the state of affairs least favorable to connecting the sound *üg* with that shell.

Let his prattling possibilities consist of a thousand syllables all equally likely to occur, and all as likely to occur in any one situation as in any other. Then the chance that he will utter *üg* as he puts a pebble in the shell is 1 in 1000 if he prattles at all. And unless that connection between the manual act and the vocal act is somehow strengthened, he will be as likely the next time that he drops a pebble into that shell to utter any other sound in his repertoire as to utter *üg*. Very often he will utter other sounds and no progress will be made toward the attachment of meanings to his utterances.

But there are forces which tend to cause progress away from purely miscellaneous vocal play. First of all the child who puts one pebble in the shell is likely to put another in then and there. His enjoyment of the act makes him repeat it, that is, strengthens its connection with the mental set in which he did it first. Now that mental set happened at that time to evoke also the vocal play of saying *üg*, and the confirming reaction which the enjoyment of the manual play set in action tends to spread or scatter so as to strengthen also the connection of the situation with the utterance.

In the second place, saying *üg* to the shell and pebble may be itself enjoyable and the connection may thereby be strengthened. Consequently the probability that the child will drop a second pebble is substantial and the probability that he will utter *üg* therewith if he utters anything is far above 1 in 1000.

Let us assume provisionally that some active-minded *Homo sapiens* did thus connect *ma* with the mother who nursed and fondled him, *ba* with the round black thing that rolled and tossed, *unk* with the club with which he knocked down his prey, and similarly for a dozen or more "words," as we may truly call them. If he did this, what would be the probability that some second person in the group would come to understand these words? And if he did come to understand them, what would be the probability that the first person would come to use them with the intent of having the second person understand them, and so attain the condition of possessing speech as a social tool?

If one person in a hitherto languageless group of

two or three dozen souls has reached the stage of a private language of a score of words the probability that some other person in the group will come to understand three or four of his words is much more than infinitesimal.

His companions might well hear him say *kuz* as he dug up a clam or opened a clam or ate a clam, a hundred times in a week. Even if they paid no more attention to his speech than to his personal play, vocal or non-vocal, the sound *kuz* would tend to make them think of a clam more often than of any other one object. And under certain conditions they would be attentive to his speech. For example, in a group digging for clams together, if one cried *kuz* whenever he found a clam, the cry would become interesting to others.

If the group had a dozen or so "bow-wow" (that is, mimetic) words that they used as signals, they would be thereby the more disposed to attend each to the other's vocalizations. If a second person of the group had a private language of his own, though unlike that of the first person in every particular, the second person would be thereby the more disposed to attend to the first person's vocalizations. If the group had a system of mutual influence by gestures, even one utterly devoid of any vocal accompaniments, its members would be thereby a little more disposed to attend to the vocal behavior one of another.

So I would set the probability that in a group of thirty souls, one of whom had a private language of twenty words, some one other person would come to understand five of these words in the course of a moderate lifetime of thirty-five years as well above one in ten thousand, and probably above one in a thousand.

If the family group of say thirty souls has an inventor of a private language of say twenty-five words and say ten of the thirty understand say eight of the words, what is the probability that any one of these ten will use any of the eight words that he understands, use it, that is, to mean to himself the thing or act or event in question, so as to aid him, for example, in planning to dig clams? This probability is substantial, but it is not 100 out of 100. Some persons in such a group will hear and understand a word hundreds of times, but in all probability never say it at all, except accidentally as an element in their meaningless chatter. But some will, when they themselves utter this word in their meaningless chatter or for any reason, understand it as if it were spoken by A. And this act of saying a word and having it mean something will tend to be satisfying rather than annoying. Meaningful prattle is more satisfying that meaningless and will therefore be more frequently repeated.

If A, the original inventor, hears B or C or D say one of the words to which he, A, attaches meaning when he himself says them, what is the probability that he, A, will understand the word spoken by B? It is not 100 out of 100. The connection *kuz→clam* may remain confined to *kuz* said by A, because A is stupid, or by nature an extreme introvert, or what William James called a lonely thinker, or because of the general tendency of connections to operate only in the way in which they are formed. But A has, by hypothesis, an I.Q. of 100 or better, and if B goes about saying *kuz* repeatedly and as if he meant something, A is likely to notice what B says, and will at least be more likely to attach the thought of *clam* to the sound *kuz* when made by B than to attach any other one meaning to it. I should conjecture that the probability of A's understanding B would be well over 25 in 100 and under 90 in 100.

It is perhaps time to attach a name to the theory which I am expounding. Let us save everybody trouble by giving it an opprobrious name from the start! Since it relies on the miscellaneous vocal play of man instead of his alleged mimetic or emotional utterances, it could be called the "babble-babble" theory. Since it starts with languages private to single persons, and progresses gradually toward speech in the full speaker-hearer relation (which, indeed, my exposition has not yet reached) it could be called the "onety-twoty" theory. Since it depends on successive selections of chance variations in sound-reality connections, it could be called the "chancy-chance" or "luck-luck" theory. Or we may combine its two main dynamic features and call it the "babble-luck" theory.

Let us continue with the luck-luck course of the babble-luck theory.

If B understands *kuz* as spoken used by A and A

understands *kuz* as spoken by B, what is the probability that A will come to use the word as a means of influencing B? What is the probability that B will come to use the word to influence A?

It is not 100 out of 100. A and B might continue for years to get meaning from one another's use of the word, but never use it for any purpose other than as a self-reminder or as an aid in personal plans, or for self-entertainment. However, if A said *kuz* when he was about to set forth to dig clams, and B was moved by hearing *kuz* to set forth to dig clams also, and so accompanied A, on several occasions, there might fairly easily be built up a habit in A of saying *kuz* when he wanted B's company on a clamming trip. (The formation of this habit would not be as simple as this sounds or by one direct linking, but by various coöperating associative links which I could describe if necessary.) Or if A had already a habit of purposive communication with B by means of a gesture such as pointing to a clam and to B's mouth when he wished or permitted B to eat it, A might well happen to say *kuz* along with the two gestures and eventually in place of the former gesture. (Here again the substitution would not be as simple as it sounds, but it could come to pass.)

A and B thus reach a stage where a word is used by one of them, say by A, with the expectation that his saying it in the presence of the other will produce or favor certain behavior in the other, and where A has the habit of saying it to the other as an appropriate thing to do when a certain desire or purpose moves him. This is genuine human language used in the speaker-hearer relation. But the relation is, as yet, undirectional, from A as speaker to B as hearer.

Speech need not progress further to full two-way, give-and-take speech, but it could, and often would. I will not run the risk of wearying you with the probabilities that the normal operations of repetition and reward would lead men to this final stage. They are high.

Each of the stages that I have described from that of words used privately to purposive use of speech in the full speaker-hearer relation was self-sustaining, by adding something to the group's balance of satisfactions. A one-man language could make that man remember, anticipate, and plan better. In so far as others understood A's words, each of them had some profit from A's experience in addition to their own. In so far as they used his words, each had a private language without originating it. When they reached the stage of understanding one another, certain experiences of any one were of profit to all. The stage of purposive use of words to modify the behavior of another gave the possibility of increasing costless coöperation and decreasing costly interference of person with person. Even if the words used were few and the occasions of their use limited to a very narrow round of suggestions, commands, invitations, and reports, the benefits would still be enough to maintain the linguistic activities.

Nothing in all this so far requires that either A or B think of the other as imagining or meaning clams when he says *kuz*. Such imputation of an inner life to another may arise later and regardless of communication, though of course it cannot progress far without communication. How it arises is a fascinating problem, but to discuss it would make for too long an interruption of our present task.

Let us turn rather to some possible criticisms. First it will be said that the speech which I have derived from babble by luck is a pitifully small, crude affair in comparison with the speech of any known group present or past. This criticism is true. Even after a dozen or more words had been used purposively hundreds of times by a third of the family group and understood after a fashion by two thirds of the group, the use and understanding would be nowhere nearly as clean-cut as that of a modern man or child. A person could use words more or less appropriately in certain situations in the sense that the use of the word was much more appropriate on the average than saying nothing, or than saying some other word of those in his active vocabulary. He could understand words in the sense that what he did to the total situation including the word was on the average different from what he would have done if some other word had been there, and better than what he would have done if no word had been there. But when the imperfect appropriateness of a speaker's uses was combined with a hearer's inadequate understandings, a perfect result could not be expected. If the speaker went much beyond the regular routine uses, he would arouse misunderstanding, neglect, or perplexity. The group's linguistic activities might be clumsy as well as extremely narrow.

It will be said that the evolution of any language worthy of the name from such crude beginnings is problematic. This criticism also is true, but it is not very damaging. The problems are no harder than the problems of the evolution of mechanical tools from their crude beginnings. The evolution of a vocabulary of two hundred names of acts, objects, and events from a vocabulary of twenty is a problem, though a rather easy one.[3] The evolution of a language that can mean qualities and relations as well as objects and events is a further problem. The evolution of a language that can by sounds ask questions, distinguish orders from statements, and date events has further problems. Refinements of meaning, as by our adjectives and adverbs, and abbreviations of speech as by our pronouns, involve further problems.

I have not solved these and other problems. But I think they are all soluble. If the facts which I have related account for how men came to use articulate words with the purpose of influencing other men, to

[3] One generation having reached the linguistic status I have described, the second generation can learn from it and spend most of its linguistic activity in adding its inventions to the parental stock. The custom of naming things and acts by sounds may, after a certain number of such sound→meaning connections has been reached, become a conscious deliberate habit. Some early linguist may then devote his spare time to naming every person in the group, every animal that frequents the locality, and every tool or weapon that he uses.

understand such words, and to coöperate in the speaker-hearer relation, they can fairly be said to account for the *origin* of language, but to leave us with many problems of its *development*.

A third possible criticism is that the babble-luck doctrine should have produced dozens, maybe hundreds, of different languages of this beggarly sort. Origin from miscellaneous babble would cause multiplicity of primeval languages unless one family group got so great a head start that its language spread to all other tribes before they had invented any language of their own, which is unlikely. I see nothing objectionable in this. It seems to me sure that any continuing group of intelligent human beings would in time get a language from babble and luck if they did not get it earlier from neighbors or visitors who already had it. In many cases they would get it so. Inter-group learning would be of the same general nature as the intra-group learning.

A fourth possible criticism is that hundreds of generations seem to be required to get even this beggerly language if the group has no aid from outside. This seems to be really an argument *pro* rather than *con*. Surely the notion that primeval men who were wordless get words as quickly as modern men get Mohammedanism or Christianity or steam engines is fantastic. The length of time from selecting and using flints that were sharp to chipping flints to make them sharp, and the length of time from chipping them roughly to chipping and polishing them in the elegant neolithic styles, are both reckoned in many thousands of years.

Whatever may be the value of this account of the origin of meaningful speech, one thing is certain. The human animal's miscellaneous play with his vocal apparatus, and the articulate sounds he thereby produces, and the associations he makes of these with things and events independently of, and especially contrary to, his linguistic environment, deserve much more attention from psychology and linguistic science than they have hitherto received.

## VI

## THE PSYCHOLOGY OF GOVERNMENT:
## RULERS AND RULED

T HE ESSENTIAL FACTS OF GOVERNMENT are rules
and rulers. In this country the rules are consti-
tutions, federal, state, and municipal statutes, and
principles of the common law; and the rulers are
Presidents, Governors, Mayors, legislative bodies, the
courts, various administrative bodies, and the army,
navy, police, and civil services. Governing implies
actual or possible coercion of the ruled by the rulers.
The rulers are selected by majorities of voters, directly or indirectly, and in theory are public servants
through whom majorities of voters rule themselves
and their fellow men.

The theory is that in a democracy the will of the
people streams forth through a system of human con-
ductors to have its way in the world. In a pure
monarchy, the theory is that government expresses
automatically the will of the king or czar, and in a
pure democracy government expresses automatically
the will of the people. The facts are very different.
A Peter or Louis of old, or a dictator of today, is a
man whose will operates in the form of his own acts,
chiefly commands, and through an organization of
subordinate rulers, on a population habituated to a
regime of rights and privileges hallowed by custom.

His will is supported by promises and threats, which are supported in turn by rewards and punishments. Even though his subjects consider him divine or possessed of magic powers, he is in fact a man. Like any man his will may fail of its object because his acts are inadequate, because his executive officers are unable or unwilling to fulfill his commands, or because his subjects are unable or unwilling to fulfill the commands which they receive. Moreover, what he thinks is his will may be, in whole or in part, the will of favorites, courtiers, or bureaucrats inoculated into his mind, a perversion of his real will.

In a democracy the will of the majority operates by means of, or at times in spite of, parties, party bosses, committees and active members, blocs or pressure groups, the press, and other human apparatus for choosing and instructing representatives. The representatives operate by means of, or in spite of, coalitions, blocs, trading, propaganda, and various less creditable influences. Their decisions are carried out by armies, navies, policemen, judges, and other public servants in so far as these are able and willing. The complexity of the process has a familiar illustration in the enactment and enforcement of local and nation-wide prohibition laws, especially the Volstead Act, in the United States.

Even in a small city state or a simple pastoral tribe, the will of either an alleged absolute ruler or a majority of members acts under similar, if less elaborate, restrictions. Indeed even the simplest known government, the matriarchy of a single child by its mother, is not entirely devoid of psychological complexities! The mother's will, though supported by complete physical control, does not always have its way.

I propose to state some of the psychological facts about rules, rulers, and ruled, representation, representatives, and citizens, promises, threats, and coercion, which influence government and influence especially the contributions of government to welfare.

I must now rectify an omission which may have shocked many of you. The orthodox beginning for any discussion of government is to quote Aristotle's dictum that "Man is by nature a political animal." I hope the delay in introducing these sacred words has not annoyed or perplexed you. They have misled many into attributing to all men at all times an active interest in public affairs and government and a rather high degree of ability to coöperate for the welfare of a tribe, city, or nation.

By original nature man is not a political animal to that extent. He had to learn to live in and carry on a city state, as truly as he had to learn to use the Greek alphabet in writing, or to use money as a medium of exchange. Politics and government are no more natural and gene-determined than religion, education, manufacturing, or trade. Man's genes do provide certain probabilities of responses to the behavior of other human beings which, under certain conditions, favor the survival of the human family, tribe, or other human group of which the man is a member. These original social instincts seem to be approximately as follows:

*Gregariousness.* The continued absence of human beings causes discomfort and restlessness; their presence, a positive satisfaction. The presence of a large number is, other things being equal, especially exhilarating.

*Giving attention.* The behavior of other human beings has an original interest for men and still more for women. The circumstances of life maintain and increase this.

*Responses by approval and scorn.* By nature, we smile, look admiringly, and shout encouragingly at those who feed us when we are hungry, banish our fears, act with notable strength and daring, win physical victories, or make a gorgeous display. Frowns, hoots, jeers, sneers, and spittings are the portion of those who are empty-handed, deformed, pusillanimous, or mean.

*Responses to approval and scorn.* Acceptance, smiles, pats, and the like from superiors and equals, and the humbler approval just described from anyone, cause satisfaction. Rejection by superiors and equals, and hoots, jeers, and sneers from any one cause discomfort. In some sensitive souls the satisfaction and discomfort may be extreme.

*Mastery and submission.* The genes provide man with two mutually exclusive sets of responses which may compete or alternate, and which make various combinations with fighting, fears, affection, and other strands of behavior. A typical response of mastery or domination is to hold the head up and forward, staring at the person to be mastered, looking him in the eye, making various displays of strength, and perhaps shoving him, and grabbing any food or other desirable that he holds. A typical response of submission is a bowing of the head, cowering of the body, wavering glance, absence of all preliminaries of attack, general weakening of muscle tonus, and hesitancy in movements. This response is aroused by attempts at mastery in a person who is notably large and energetic, or who inflicts blows on us at will. When mastery fails to exact submission there is typically a conflict of looks, gestures, or actual attacks until the submission of one party or the exhaustion of both. By the genes every pair of associated human beings thus tends to reach a more or less permanent status of dominance and submission, and even in modern environments something of this often persists.

*Motherly behavior.* "All women possess originally, from early childhood to death, some interest in human babies, and a responsiveness to the instinctive looks, calls, gestures and cries of infancy and childhood, being satisfied by childish gurglings, smiles and affectionate gestures, and moved to instinctive comforting acts by childish signs of pain, grief and misery. . . . Brutal habits may destroy, or competing habits overgrow, or the lack of exercise weaken, these tendencies, but they are none the less as original as any fact in human nature." [1]

Gregariousness and the tendencies to attention-getting and giving keep a band of humans together

[1] Thorndike, *Original Nature of Man*, p. 81 f., *passim.*

and make each sensitive to the abilities and wants of others. The mastery-submission tendencies can give organization to a small roving band and status to each member of it. The approval-disapproval tendencies favor the particular forms of conduct specified, and in general favor conformity to any custom which for any reason has been approved by the masters in the group. Maternal behavior can become a more general humanitarianism exercised upon the weak or injured within the group, which is a step of advance toward a conception of group welfare and responsibility. Childless women have been scorned in most civilizations, but they may have played an important role as mothers and nurses to the group.

Even before a human group had a well-developed language, these tendencies, as modified by the forces of repetition and reward, could cause a man to enjoy his group's assemblies, ceremonies, and other joint enterprises, and to be interested in, and take satisfaction from, his group's perceived successes. They help make him what may be called a communal animal, but hardly a political animal in any useful sense of the word. That he could hardly become until language had developed sufficiently to enable one person to give many and various orders to another, and two or more persons to agree on many facts, purposes, and plans.

These forces bred in the genes are, and always have been, potent in man's behavior, and perhaps have counted more in his political behavior than in his domestic or business behavior, but they did not alone create it. Indeed some of the most important features of government are decidedly alien to them. For example, government by an oligarchy of the old males was widespread early and long. The genes do not make adults revere or obey the aged. They make the weak revere and obey the strong, and consequently make the child and young adolescent seek protection, help, and advice from vigorous adults.[2]

In Aristotle's day the citizens of the city states that he knew were not only communal animals but political persons. Each of them was aware of his tribal group as having public interests and activities beyond and above getting food and making love; and was aware of it, or certain rulers in it, as exercising coercion upon individuals, beyond and above the coercion of individual upon individual. Similarly, men and women in civilized nations today are with few exceptions poiltical persons. They use the words *public* and *government* freely. They distinguish public from private affairs, though of course not infallibly or unanimously. They feel that they do or should belong to their town, not merely reside in it, that they belong to England, Sweden, the United States, or the like, and that it belongs to them. A great majority of adult citizens of the United States are aware of at least some of the things that local, state,

[2] The mental connections, formed in infancy, childhood, and early youth toward certain fathers and uncles persist so that men of forty revere and obey the weak graybeards of seventy. Also, in a civilization that is changing very slowly and has no written repositories of knowledge, the aged have

and federal governments do, and have some interest in some of these things.

The fact that we are by nature such communal animals, and by nature plus experience such political persons, does not get political science very far in explaining good government and bad government, the history of government, or its future course.

Nor do any other facts and principles of psychology do very much for political science. Psychologists did no better than historians or economists or sociologists in predicting the political convulsions of our generation. And what I have to offer to you is only selections from a miscellany of psychological notes about citizens, rulers, and rules, which are little in advance of common knowledge.

Let us begin with citizens and with their desire to govern themselves. It is very weak. Men like to have things their own way, but most men do not like to think, contrive, and labor to get them so. Everyone in this audience, for example, knows that he will have a very small share in local, state, or national government if he does not attend his party's primaries regularly, but how many of you do that? The Athenian Greeks were notably politically minded and patriotic, but we are told that after a time they had to be paid to attend the assembly and vote. We may enjoy politics as spectators enjoy a game or conflict, but

---

the asset of greater experience. They may remember how the group got out of a certain difficulty that has not occurred for fifty years. Reliance on their knowledge may be preserved as well as established by repetition and reward.

few of us actually play the game and still fewer work to learn it and keep in training for it.

Government involves responsibility and coöperation (in novel situations in both cases). The enjoyment of these is rare. So citizens let themselves be ruled by the few who are willing to take the responsibility and do the work — professional politicians, a governing class, or a dictator.

Consider next the interest of citizens in public affairs. This too is slight except when the public affair has an obvious influence on their private affairs, or has dramatic appeal. So a proposal that government pay thirty dollars a month to persons over sixty will arouse interest in sexagenarians. And a duel in the form of a presidential election will arouse a few months' interest every four years. But these are really cases of interest in private affairs and in entertaining events. A fair measure of the interest in public affairs is given by the behavior of citizens toward public property. They do not greatly cherish it, nor try to increase it, nor reward those who do increase it, nor even think much about it. The apathy of the great majority of citizens toward public debts is even greater.

Psychologically these lacks of participation and interest are explainable. The path of least resistance for a citizen is to get a living by some work that he enjoys and to spend the balance of his time in being entertained. Since the politicians and newspapers treat him with respect whenever they talk to him or about him, he feels no annoying lack of power. On the contrary he can think comfortably that his vote counts just as much as a millionaire's or a general's; and he can feel that he has a right to make demands of his congressman. He can have much of the exaltation of power with little labor or strain. If he does try to take an active part in government the consequences are rarely satisfying enough to confirm the practice. Both repetition and reward favor passivity.

So far as concerns interest, why should he search into the facts of government until he has exhausted the much more interesting facts of the fortunes of himself, his family, and his friends, any more than he should search into the facts of geology? The search would involve thought, to which man is averse, and its consequences would more often be a headache than a pleasant surprise or gratifying insight. Let the facts of government wait until they are in the headlines; let geology wait until there is an earthquake! The reason why what is anybody's and everybody's business becomes nobody's business is that people in general are not often moved to undertake it and do not often get satisfying consequences when they do undertake it.

Consider next the psychology of patriotism toward one's town, state, or nation, especially toward one's nation, and take as an introduction to the topic the bitter, not to say venomous, analysis by Veblen:

> The patriotic spirit is a spirit of emulation, evidently, at the same time that it is emulation shot through with a sense of solidarity. It belongs under the general caption of sportsmanship, rather than of workmanship. Now,

any enterprise in sportsmanship is bent on an invidious success, which must involve as its major purpose the defeat and humiliation of some competitor, whatever else may be comprised in its aim. . . .

Patriotism is evidently a spirit of particularism, of aliency and animosity between contrasted groups of persons; it lives on invidious comparison, and works out in mutual hindrance and jealousy between nations. It commonly goes the length of hindering intercourse and obstructing traffic that would patently serve the material and cultural well-being of both nationalities; and not infrequently, indeed normally, it eventuates in competitive damage to both. . . .

Into the culture and technological system of the modern world the patriotic spirit fits like dust in the eyes and sand in the bearings. Its net contribution to the outcome is obscuration, distrust, and retardation at every point where it touches the fortunes of modern mankind. Yet it is forever present in the counsels of the statesmen and in the affections of the common man, and it never ceases to command the regard of all men as the prime attribute of manhood and the final test of the desirable citizen. It is scarcely an exaggeration to say that no other consideration is allowed in abatement of the claims of patriotic loyalty, and that such loyalty will be allowed to cover any multitude of sins.[3]

There is much truth in Veblen's diatribe. To desire and enjoy the success of our nation does often make us desire and enjoy the failure of other nations. To work and sacrifice for our nation often goes with action against other nations. Patriotic loyalty may

[3] From *Inquiry into the Nature of Peace and the Terms of its Perpetuation* by Thorstein Veblen, pp. 33–40, *passim*. Copyright 1917. By permission of The Viking Press, Inc., New York.

sometimes disregard absolute welfare in its zeal for relative superiority, and even be content to drag one's own nation down if it can drag others down much more. Two competing nations may, by "patriotic" tariffs, quotas, and the like, each cut off its own nose to spite the other's face. International justice, if we could get it, would presumably be better for the world than national loyalties. Rulers probably have, consciously or unconsciously, cultivated patriotism in citizens for selfish purposes of their own. We probably do overvalue loyalty to the group in comparison with loyalty to the truth or loyalty to the right, and in comparison with honesty, justice, and kindness.

But Veblen's brilliant literary talents may easily mislead. The passage quoted may leave the reader with the belief that *un*patriotism, *dis*loyalty to the group, would be better for the world than patriotism — that objectors and rebels are much oftener right than conformists. That is nonsense. Nor are the patriotisms of the world as irrational and bigoted as Veblen says. Listen to the much more temperate and favorable description written in the same year (1917) as Veblen's, by a great rebel, Bertrand Russell, who had suffered much from patriots.

Patriotism is a very complex feeling, built up out of primitive instincts and highly intellectual convictions. There is love of home and family and friends, making us peculiarly anxious to preserve our own country from invasion. There is the mild instinctive liking for compatriots as against foreigners. There is pride, which is bound up with the success of the community to which we feel that we belong. There is a belief, suggested by pride but reinforced by history, that one's own nation represents a great tradition and stands for ideals that are important to the human race. But besides all these, there is another element, at once nobler and more open to attack, an element of worship, of willing sacrifice, of joyful merging of the individual life in the life of the nation. This religious element in patriotism is essential to the strength of the State, since it enlists the best that is in most men on the side of national sacrifice.[4]

It is not for me to try to instruct you concerning either the morality or the utility of patriotism. But I may state what seems to be the psychology of its basal fact.

National patriotism is a case of identification of ourselves with something to which we have a double relation of belonging. We belong to the United States and it belongs to us. There is membership and also proprietorship.[5]

The main consequences of the identification is that one desires and enjoys the success of the nation, and is willing to sacrifice other goods to help it succeed. There need not be anything invidious in this, unless the interest of some other nation conflicts, or is thought to conflict, with the success of

[4] Bertrand Russell, *Why Men Fight*, p. 55 f. Quoted by permission of the publishers, D. Appleton–Century Company, New York.

[5] More widely, patriotic feeling and action may become attached by ideational affiliations. A Bostonian may thus be patriotic toward his city's ball-team. A youth may thus be patriotic toward guild socialism or surrealism.

ours. There need not be anything noble in this unless our nation is itself a noble thing.

The main cause of the identification is the gain to one's sense of personal worth. We are greater and better in our own eyes as members and owners of anything important.

Let us turn now to a few notes on the psychology of rulers. The first concerns the differences between self-appointed, divinely appointed, humanly appointed, and elected rulers. These are much smaller than the logic of the facts would lead one to suppose. Logically the man who put himself in power by his own ability should be especially self-confident and intolerant of criticism and advice, while the elected officer should be least so. Logically the appointees of a king or governor or political boss should be especially loyal, and even subservient, to those who have given them power. But power tends to justify itself to its possessors regardless of whether it was given by voters, or by superiors, or by God, or by fortune, or was taken by one's own might and skill.

Psychologically, power tends toward aggrandizement and irresponsibility. Almost without exception the Presidents of the United States have magnified their office at the expense of the legislative branch. Even so modest a man as Lincoln did so, according to Dr. Small.

We noted in an earlier lecture that an extraordinarily vigorous struggle was necessary for a man to keep all his human relations in order and act with perfect appropriateness in each. The mind rebels against the thought and strain required to do this, and pressures from selfishness, conceit, and love of mastery encourage men elected or appointed as trustees of the public welfare or the interests of groups of voters to act as fathers, masters, teachers, owners, or whatever is most comfortable for them. The elected officer who desires to be reëlected may easily slip from the attitude of representing the wishes and interests of the voters into the attitude of a demagog captivating them. He may minimize his obligations to them in favor of his obligations to the party machine. He may, if self-confident and imperious, use his power to please himself, in spite of the risks in the next election. The officer appointed as the choice of some superior officer or of the machine may easily slip from gratitude, even in La Rochefoucauld's base sense of "a secret desire of receiving greater benefit," into complacency and thence into independence.

The most alluring slip is toward mastery. He who is given power tends to slip into tyranny, benevolent or otherwise. This is none the less true if he holds his power as elected representative, as trustee, or as an anointed servant of God. Psychologically most rulers are potential dictators. These and other facts lend some truth to the saying that nobody is good enough to rule his fellow men. But somebody must.

My next comment concerns the pretentious infallibility of most rulers. Why does a ruler maintain that he was right when a reasonable consideration of the facts proves clearly that he was wrong? The simplest answer is that everybody does just this so far as he can, and that a ruler can do so oftener than the rest of us because his supporters help him to avoid facing the facts. This is a good answer as far as it goes. Human minds in general care very little for truth. Much more time has been spent by mankind in fabricating entertaining and gratifying fancies than in searching for the truth. Gravitation in the mind is toward what is comforting, not toward what is true. Roughly speaking, a man seeks the truth only when it is more comfortable for him to do so than not to do so. Scientists and scholars are trained to take pride in getting the truth and are paid in money and public esteem for doing so. So they seek it diligently. Moreover, their deviations from the truth arouse the scorn of their peers. If they do make a mistake, they regain some self-esteem and esteem of their peers by acknowledging it. So it is good form in university circles to say "I conjecture that," "probably," "I do not know," and even "I was wrong." But even scientists and scholars like to cover up and forget their mistakes. Most men acknowledge them only when they would appear foolish if they did not, and not always then. We deceive ourselves to retain our self-esteem. The workman blames his tools or materials or boss. The business man blames the chain stores, or the times, or his advisors. The farmer blames the weather. Every person gravitates toward a comfortable self-esteem.

But there is more to the ruler's ostensible infallibility than this common tendency, plus an entourage of flatterers which the common man lacks. The work of a doctor, lawyer, teacher, or engineer, and still more that of a mechanic or clerk, consists largely of routines 99 per cent of which the person is competent to pursue even if he thinks about the mistakes he made the week before. Not so the varied and novel tasks of the ruler, or other high executive. His daily round of conferences and decisions would be a misery if he was harassed by thoughts of his past blunders. He would be unable to lead, persuade, and coerce if his appearance of leadership, friendliness, and power was marred by inner inhibiting fears of weakness and folly.

There is still more. A very large percentage of his acts as ruler concern appointments of persons and approvals of policies in regard to which only elaborate studies could at the time prophesy surely whether his act would turn out well or ill. In such cases, a good ruler gets the best advice he can. If the advice turns out badly, he cannot lay the blame on his advisor as you and I can lay the blame on our doctor, or lawyer, or banker. In the etiquette of government, a ruler must take the responsibility with the glory. Counting both his own mistakes and those of his advisors, even a better than average ruler is responsible for so many that if he kept track of all and publicly acknowledged them he would be making such acknowledgements morning, noon, and night! So he acknowledges none. This seems an intolerable egotism to the moralist; but the great majority of the ruled do not object to it. Those of the opposition party who clamor loudest about the ruler's blunders do not ridicule or even reproach him for not acknowledging them.

A more important problem concerning rulers is what manner of men they should be. Has psychology any suggestions about who should govern?

The answer that comes first to mind and satisfies many is "Those who can do it best," but that answer is wrong here as it is also for every feature of man's work. If each job in the world claimed the man who could do it best, Winston Churchill might have been kept as a war correspondent, Thomas Edison as a magazine vendor, Andrew Carnegie as a telegraph operator, John D. Rockefeller, Senior, as a Sunday School superintendent, his son as a Sunday School teacher, Madame Curie as a housekeeper, Shakespeare as an actor, and Aristotle as a private in the army.

Jobs should have priority ratings according to their importance. Moreover, among jobs of equal importance the allocation of men should not be so as to give to each the job he can do best, but so as to obtain the best total result. Thus if the achievements of persons A, B, C, and D in jobs 1, 2, 3, and 4 (all of equal importance) would be as shown below, the allotment of each job to the one of the four men who can do it best would be 1 to B, 2 to A, 3 to A, and 4 to A, which is not possible. The allotment of each man to the job that he can do best of the four jobs would be A to 2, B to 2, C to 3, and D to 3, which also is not possible. To maximize the total C must

have job 3, though he is the poorest of the four men
at it, and the best man for the job gets it only in the
case of jobs 1 and 4.

|  | Job 1 | Job 2 | Job 3 | Job 4 |
|---|---|---|---|---|
| Man A | 80 | 100 | 85 | 95 |
| Man B | 90 | 95 | 80 | 30 |
| Man C | 20 | 10 | 60 | 20 |
| Man D | 35 | 80 | 90 | 60 |

The best allocation is 1 to B, 2 to D, 3 to C, and
4 to A.

Psychology finds that abilities are highly specialized, so that how well a man will govern cannot be
told with surety from any estimate in advance. In
particular, men react very differently and often unexpectedly to sudden increases in power. A college
professor esteemed as genial, democratic, coöperative, and relatively modest surprised his friends upon
his appointment as the head of a large institution by
becoming a harsh, aloof autocrat. Other things being
equal, men who have been used to power over men
and money are consequently to be preferred as holders of political power.

Psychology finds that interest and ability are posi-
tively related both in the sense that the man who
likes to do a certain thing more than other men do
will do it better than they, and in the sense that the
man who likes to do a certain thing more than he
likes to do other things will do it better than he will
do them. Consequently, other things being equal,
forcing persons to take part in government as a duty

is inferior to selecting the best from those who want to govern.

Psychology finds almost no truth in the popular doctrine that men fall naturally into types, those of one type being much alike *inter se*, and all of them being very different from men of another type. Training may produce a legal type, a clerical type, a military type, an artistic type, a governing type, and the like, but the genes do not. By nature men vary in their fitness to fight, or paint, or govern, or anything else, but the variation is gradual, all degrees of fitness from the highest to near zero being found, and large numbers of men being found who are about equally well fitted for a dozen different careers. This is true of every division of minds into types that has ever been put forward, or that ever will be. It is true of E. Spranger's division into (1) the theoretical man, (2) the economic man, (3) the esthetic man, (4) the social man, (5) the man of power, and (6) the religious man.

If the life history and present status of each boy in the class of 1946 in Harvard College should be studied by Professors Allport, Boring, Dearborn, Wells, and six more of their colleagues in psychology and psychiatry, each boy being then assigned to one of the Spranger classes, probably not one boy in twenty would be put in the same class by all ten judges, and many a boy would be put in all six classes. The Spranger system would in fact work better for Harvard's buildings than for its students! Emerson Hall can be a theoretical building. The Coop is an economic building. Whatever it may be, Thayer Hall is not an esthetic building! We should waste our time if we tried first to sort out the men of power in order to find the best men to select to rule us. The well-known division of men into introverts and extraverts is equally misleading. Most of us are neither introverts nor extraverts, but plain verts, or neutroverts. The traditional classification into men of thought, men of feeling, and men of action is better, though it, too, does more harm than good unless used with extreme caution.

These facts of (1) vocational selection for the optimal total result, (2) the specialization of abilities, (3) the correlation of ability with interest, and (4) the arrangement of mankind with no distinct types clearly separated one from another like the chemical elements, may help in deciding the very practical questions of government by professional politicians, government by experts, and hierarchical government.

Moralists, reformers, and many writers about government scorn the professional politician, but as an honest psychologist I must speak in his defense. He keeps at the work and has a record on the job so that we can judge what he will do by what he has done. It is our fault if we keep him on. He does the work from interest; his contribution to the welfare of the world in some other capacity is not likely to be much greater. Is not the scorn of the high-minded partly undeserved? Is it not in part our defense-reaction when he beats us in the game of politics? Is it not in part a matter of other qualities which happen to accompany earning a living in politics and government? If professional politicians are more stupid, selfish, dishonest, and vicious than professional preachers, engineers, or teachers of political science, they are, in so far forth, more deserving of scorn. But would they deserve less if they turned from their work at politics and preached sermons or taught political science?

Is not part of the scorn an unjustifiable idealism which demands a world in which St. Pauls preach without pay, Spinozas philosophize without pay, and Darwins give their lives to science without pay? One feels uplifted as well as charmed by the thought of such a world, but in actual fact our present way is better. If you had been in control of funds in those days, you would have taken St. Paul off tents and put him preaching full time, and Spinoza would never have ground another lens after you had known of his work as a philosopher.

Government by experts is scorned by the man in the street as government by professional politicians is scorned by the high-minded, but of course for very different reasons. There are some grains of common sense in this scorn, but most of it is due to ignorance, prejudice, and the vicious habit of exalting ourselves by dragging down our betters.

The experts in question are of two sorts: (1) experts in the science of government and politics, and (2) experts in economics, law, engineering, warfare, public health, education, and other arts and sciences which concern public affairs.

Experts of the first sort, such as the professors of government in our universities, are not very expert. They would themselves admit it, and contrast their science with that of an astronomer, or chemist, or electrical engineer. They do not know the facts about governments nearly as completely and accurately as chemists know the facts about chemicals. It is in so far forth sensible to prefer men of affairs, or practical politicians (or statesmen, if there is any difference) to masters of political science. The latter are also presumably very useful where they are, have not demonstrated that they possess the specialized abilities of a good ruler in high degree, and have no great interest in ruling. For these reasons also there is a grain of sense in preferring men of affairs or practical politicians.

But most of the scorn is caused, not by sensible considerations, but by people's ignorance of the important contributions that the sciences of government and of management in general could make, by their prejudice against whatever is unfamiliar and unintelligible to them, and by their short-sighted proclivity to make themselves comfortable for the moment at great cost to their total welfare. In my childhood the expert in agricultural science was treated with similar scorn, and for similar reasons. It is easy and comforting to think that nobody is much wiser or abler than you are, or could be if you wished. So a proposal that the most eminent professor of government in the United States should be chosen to be its President would arouse a chorus of jeers. I hap-

pen to have known only three professors of government at all well, but I dare to assert that any one of
the three would have made a better President than
some that our country did choose. The same psychology is at work in the reluctance to let economists,
engineers, or biologists rule, but it is tempered by
wider acceptance of the facts that these experts are
masters of knowledges and skills that we lack and
that are of great importance to welfare.

A solution that puts expert abilities at the service
of the public and at the same time makes voters,
professional politicians, and men of affairs comfortable is to put these experts under somebody who is
not an expert. This works fairly well if the superior
officer prudently confines himself to reconciling and
adjusting the acts and recommendations of the various experts under him, and emphasizes his functions
as organizer and coördinator. But it works badly if
he favors the persons and acts that he happens to
like, vetoes recommendations that he dislikes, commands the experts as a sergeant commands a squad
of soldiers or as a foreman commands workman, and
in general emphasizes the relation of superior to
subordinate.

Business and industry are outgrowing the latter
attitude. Management is becoming functional rather
than hierarchical. The top executive is becoming a
coördinator rather than a boss. The effort is to have
final decisions made by the person best qualified to
make them, not by the person highest in authority.
In some organizations the expert does not have to

persuade and coax. He is vetoed only by genuine conflict of his proposals with interests which other experts and the general management must protect. He is not a servitor at the beck and call of the top executive. Indeed the top executive in a modern functional organization may with some truth say that he is a mixture of one third father-confessor, one third judge, and one third errand-boy for his legal department, finance department, production department, sales department, and research department. Should not government learn from business administration? Should not a government be much more a board of coöperating experts, and much less a hierarchy of bosses?

## VII

## THE PSYCHOLOGY OF GOVERNMENT:
## LAWS AND THE LAW

ALMOST ALL EARLY LAWS originated in the customs or mores of communities, and established punishments for the violation of these. Even so late as the eighteenth century, Lord Mansfield incorporated the useful and reasonable customs of business men into the general body of the law of England. And in our own day, much legislation concerning public health, public education, and automobile traffic has adopted customs that already controlled the more prudent and better informed. Consequently it would be in order to relate the psychology of these long-lived popular habits in which for ages man has embodies his ideas and ideals. I shall, however, restrict the statement of facts about customs to those which should be in mind in order to evaluate the rules or laws by which customs are approved for universal use and enforced.

The customs of groups, like the habits of individuals, are maintained chiefly by repetition and reward. I think that there is also a growing satisfyingness of the familiar course of action for no other reason than its familiarity. The only experiments on this point that I know of gave positive results.[1] And

[1] Reported in 1937, in the *Journal of Experimental Psychology*, XXI, 162–180.

many of you prefer sitting in your accustomed chair, though you would have preferred some other chair had you habitually sat in it. But the causation of such a potency of familiarity is mysterious, and it would be a bit risky for the government of either states or families to rely upon the principle that familiarity breeds not contempt, but content. Customary acts are usually rewarded in less mysterious ways. It is easier not to change; a failure of a course of action to complete its usual round brings a slight irritation or disappointment; the custom was started because it brought more satisfaction than the possible alternatives; it may have brought the reward indirectly, as when eating any food brings the satisfaction of relief from hunger and a comfortably filled stomach.

The great satisfactions brought by following the customs of the group are, however, not these minor ones, but the inner sense of worth, a good conscience arising from having done what is fit and proper, and the approval of others openly manifested or known to exist. Custom rules men but approval rules custom. If violation of a custom is applauded by those whose good opinion men crave, neither age nor sanctity will save it. Any law embodying it and punishing departures from it will be repealed, left unenforced, or make offenders into martyrs.

Consider now the very common case where a law is a rule sanctioning a certain custom and arranging for the punishment of those who act contrary to it, asking especially "What psychological good does it do, more than the custom alone did?" When the laws of the Twelve Tables stated "If a man kills his parent, veil his head, sew him up in a sack, and throw him into the river," what gain was there over the customary treatment of patricides and matricides which presumably antedated the law?

For the argument's sake let us suppose that the law parallels the custom perfectly, not adding a jot or subtracting a tittle. The law could still be useful psychologically in several ways. First, it can be informative. Those who have never witnessed or heard of the custom in question can get an adequate idea of it; they certainly can from the admirably brief and straightforward statement of our illustration. Rules publicize customs. Second, it may be committed to memory more easily. Actual instances of customs, their violation, and the consequent punishment are superior to the corresponding rules in vividness, but they are rare in experience and are not, or were not before moving-picture cameras, easy to reproduce. Laws or other verbal rules preserve the memory of customs, and so help to preserve the customs themselves.

Third, rules can be more definite and exact than customs are likely to be. Even the most familiar and stereotyped custom will, if left alone, vary somewhat with the past experiences and present attitudes of the persons involved. Even the most stable custom will, if left alone, shift somewhat with time and circumstance. Practice under the control of custom alone may vary or even become chaotic, but a rule in words says what it says, and is unchanged except for changes in the meanings of its words. On the assumption that the preservation of customs is desirable, customs plus rules are in so far forth better than customs alone.

Fourth, laws suggest that it is somebody's particular business to attend to their enforcement. Customs operate largely through a miscellaneous public. Arrangement for officers of the law were coincident with, if not a necessary accompaniment of, the formulation of laws. The laws of the Twelve Tables, for example, refer specifically to the praetor. All modern laws, of course, assume courts and lawyers and agents and apparatus to put the decisions of the courts into effect. Laws thus exemplify a specialization and division of labor as compared with customs.

Laws produce customs as truly, though not as often, as customs produce laws. Even in early times the powerful may have made rules and created customs of obeying these rules by rewarding obedience. And in modern times a common procedure of those who wish to start some custom is to try to get a law passed requiring it, or favoring it. Nor do they waste their time. Say what you please about the need of educating the public to want a law before enacting it, the psychologist who wanted to start a custom, say of having a competent psychologist attached as advisor to every children's court, would get a law to that effect enacted as soon as he could by honorable means. He would reckon on the inertia of the great majority of citizens concerning any *fait accompli* in such matters, and on their reverence for law in general, rather than on the probability of arousing a widespread rational demand for this desirable psychological service. Federal, state, and municipal statutes may not do a half or a quarter of what is expected of them from their advocates, and their main service may be to spread further customs already established among the better or wiser or more informed citizens, but they are none the less a great creative force in human life.

THE LAW

Dealing as it does mainly with human behavior, the law very likely has more to teach psychology than to learn from it. The law has had a long history and very able students and practitioners. If I knew its doctrines and practices well enough I would perhaps report to you concerning what they do teach psychology. But I am better qualified for the converse task of stating facts known to psychology that may be of service to legislators, courts, and students of law.

The law has a fundamental psychology of its own, simple and brief enough to be presented in a few minutes all by quotations from Sir James Fitzjames Stephen, eminent as a lawyer and judge, and a master of exposition. So far as I know, more recent writers would say much the same. It will seem to most of you an antiquated and indefensible faculty psychology.

VOLUNTARY ACTIONS BY A PERSON FREE FROM COMPUL-SION. — In order that an act may be criminal it must be a voluntary act done by a person free from certain forms of compulsion. In explaining this proposition (which may appear to some persons to be tautological) the following terms must be considered: "action," "voluntary," "free," "compulsion". . . .

An action then is a motion or more commonly a group of related motions of different parts of the body. Actions may be either involuntary or voluntary, and an involuntary action may be further subdivided according as it is or is not accompanied by consciousness. Instances of involuntary actions are to be found not only in such motions as the beating of the heart and the heaving of the chest, but in many conscious acts — coughing, for instance, the motions which a man makes to save himself from falling, and an infinite number of others. Many acts are involuntary and unconscious, though as far as others are concerned they have all the effects of conscious acts, as, for instance, the struggles of a person in a fit of epilepsy. The classification of such actions belongs more properly to physiology than to law. For legal purposes it is enough to say that no involuntary action, whatever effects it may produce, amounts to a crime by the law of England. . . .

Such being the nature of an action, a voluntary action is a motion or group of motions accompanied or preceded by volition and directed towards some object. Every such action comprises the following elements — knowledge, motive, choice, volition, intention; and thoughts, feelings, and motions, adapted to execute the intention. These elements occur in the order in which I have enumerated them. Suppose a person about to act. His knowledge of the world in which he lives and of his own powers assures him that he can if he likes do any one or more of a certain number of things, each of which will affect him in a certain definite way, desirable or undesirable. He can speak or be silent. He can sit or stand. He can read or write. He can keep quiet or change his position to a greater or less extent and by a variety of different means. The reasons for and against these various courses are the motives. They are taken into consideration and compared together in the act of choice, which means no more than the comparison of motives. Choice leads to determination to take some particular course, and this determination issues in a volition, a kind of crisis of which everyone is conscious, but which it is impossible to describe otherwise than by naming it, and as to the precise nature and origin of which many views have been entertained which I need not here discuss. The direction of conduct towards the object chosen is called the intention or aim (for the metaphor involved in the word is obviously taken from aiming with a bow and arrow). Finally there take place a series of bodily motions and trains of thought and feeling fitted to the execution of the intention.

Whatever controversies there may be as to the nature of human beings and as to the freedom of the will, I do not think that there can be any question that this is a substantially correct account of normal voluntary action. It would be difficult to attach any meaning to the expression "voluntary action" if either motive or choice, or a volition, or an intention, or actions directed towards its execution were absent, though they may not always be equally well marked. . . .[2]

No psychologist of today would accept this as sound and adequate science. Probably neither James nor Wundt would have accepted it as sound and

[2] Sir James Fitzjames Stephen, *A History of the Criminal Law of England*, edition of 1883, II, 97–101, *passim*.

adequate science sixty years ago. Why did the law of Stephen's day retain it, in spite of what James, Wundt, and others had written? Why does the law retain it now in spite of the fact that it does not tally with what the lawyers and judges learn in even elementary courses in psychology?

The reason is, I think, that these rather archaic definitions of action, voluntary, involuntary, intention, the will, motive, choice, etc., and propositions concerning them are not, and never were, really essential to the law, but are, and were, mainly decorative. The psychology which the law really used and uses is a simple behaviorism as follows: The law requites certain persons for certain behavior, forbidden by it, using punishments, damages, and the like. The behavior has to be such as can be proved to have occurred. The person has to be responsible in the sense that if anybody should be requited, he is the one who should be, and in the sense that if he is requitable for any behavior he is requitable for this behavior. Any person's behavior is divisible into (a) that for which the law will requite him and (b) that for which it will not. The law has rules and customs for making such a division.

This psychology, which adjusts man's nature conveniently to the needs of courts and lawyers, is then decorated with terms and distinctions from theology and rather antiquated psychology, samples of which you have heard in the paragraphs from Stephen, to give the impression that the law is founded on everlasting truths of human nature. I do not criticize the law for preferring its convenient psychology to what psychologists would offer it, but I wish it would leave off the pretentious decorations.

Critics of the law, from within as well as from without, object to the law's uses of its essential psychology, as well as to the decorations. The law makes sharp divisions of mankind into two classes, they say, when there is really a continuous variation, as in intelligence or sanity. There is no gap between the most intelligent of those whom courts have declared to be idiots and the least intelligent of those whom courts have declared to be non-idiots. Mental age, the critic will continue, is much superior to chronological age for almost all purposes of the law, and should replace it as a criterion for fitness to be at large, to vote, to be a trustee or guardian, to serve on a jury, et cetera. Why does not the law in general, says the critic, consider each individual person as children's courts are permitted to do? More generally, if law is a science it should reckon with facts of biology, psychology, and other sciences of man, not the traditions of theology or even of law itself.

A gifted psychologist, E. S. Robinson, in a book entitled *Law and the Lawyers*, pleads for a study of the institutions and activities of the law in the spirit and by the methods of the natural sciences. Observation and experimentation with prediction and control as the tests of truth should, he argues, supplement, and often replace, analysis tested by consistency and so-called logic. He is confident that the opposing doctrines that law as a science is normative and that law as an application of science is an application of ethics are probably often in error and always inadequate, and that, if they were not, it still would be worth while to try studying law as we study engineering, medicine, education, and business, and to study all of these as we study atoms, bacteria, habits, and wants. I quote a few of his comments.

The man best fitted to guide us in our reform of legal institutions is he who has given frankest consideration to what that institution is as a natural phenomenon. . . . In a scientific jurisprudence *stare decisis* would stand simply for a general timidity upon the part of judges against changing their way of thinking. . . . The *ratio decidendi* of a case would be simply the best possible psychological account of why the court came to its decision. . . . The courts sometimes evoke the most mystifying concepts simply in order to do the sensible thing and to do it quickly and neatly. . . . If law should ever be considered naturistically by the professors and the books, the art of compromise could be faced more squarely. Suppressive and repressive devices could be studied, not as logically inevitable outcomes of conflict, but as drastic mechanisms to be used in social control with something of that thoughtfulness and caution with which a well-trained physician prescribes the soporific drug or the surgical extirpation.[3]

I shall not argue the merits of these criticisms. But they may introduce us to certain instructive facts.

There could be a natural science of laws, that is, of rules for men to obey, disobedience to which would

[3] From *Law and the Lawyers* by E. S. Robinson (1935), *passim*. By permission of The Macmillan Company, publishers.

be requited by governments with certain consequences. It would probably study the rules of
schools, clubs, factories, churches, armies, games,
monasteries, and many others along with the rules
now studied in law schools. It would be curious
about the consequences of rules. It would study not
only great sweeping questions such as common law
versus civil codes, popular legislation versus expert
legislation, punitive versus reformative intent, and
court law versus administrative law, but also any
consequence of any rule the study of which showed
promise of advancing knowledge. The great advances of science do not come from the study of
impressive eclipses, volcanoes, or earthquakes, but
from the study of lowly wires, magnets, scum, and
weeds. It would use experimental methods when it
could, and the mathematical analysis of variations. It
would be related to human biology, psychology, anthropology, sociology, and economics somewhat as
the science of medicine is related to physics, chemistry, biology, and botany. It would, we may conjecture, be an interesting and useful part of the
science of government.

But such a science is not what lawyers have in
mind when they speak of the law as a science. What
they have in mind is more like the science of English
grammar, or French grammar, or Greek grammar.
Men of vast learning and acute intellect have studied
and codified the various reputable and permissible
ways of using a language, and established the principles thereof, in a so-called science of its grammar.

In applying the principles of grammar one proceeds oftenest by searching for the principle or rule that decides what will be correct in the case in question. Editors and grammarians hold informal courts to decide whether certain speakings and writings are against the principles of grammar.

There is a further resemblance in the fact that changes in language require changes in grammar and changes in customs require changes in law, and that both the grammatical and legal authorities prefer to treat these as justifiable interpretations or extensions of the old principles. In both the changes are often relatively slow, so that a man can believe that his language is just the same as his father's and a judge can believe that his decisions are just the same as those his predecessor would have made. Yet in both the accumulated changes are so great that a composition written by Chaucer would not now pass a boy for college entrance and some of the routine acts of a lord of the manor in Chaucer's day would now land him promptly in jail.

The science of law that judges and lawyers now learn is this body of principles and rules, and a natural science of law, however valuable it might be, would not do the same work — would not fulfill the same function.

It is easy to see certain merits in treating individual cases after the fashion of a children's court rather than in strict adherence to classification under some general principle or rule. But the more instructive fact is the merit of the ordinary legal process.

That is prediction. The value for society of foreknowledge of what will be punished, and how, and
what can be done with impunity, of what the government will require of you and of what it will support
you in demanding from your co-citizen, and from the
alien within your gates, is so great that any institution that increases such foreknowledge has very great
value. More accurate prediction is the chief reason
(or excuse, if you prefer) for the rigidities and for-
malities of the law, for the use of law courts rather
than administrative boards, and for government by
law rather than government by men.

Perhaps we should have fewer rules. The number
of new ones enacted each year by the States and the
three hundred odd cities of 30,000 or more residents
is enormous and some of them (not many, I think)
are bad.[4] There are, I repeat, very, very few laws as
bad as this.

[4] The worst that I found in examining the statutes of four
or five cities was the following:

AN ORDINANCE PROVIDING FOR THE REGISTRATION OF
    BICYCLES BY THE OWNERS THEREOF AND FOR THE PRE-
    VENTION OF THEFT AND FOR THE DETECTION AND IDEN-
    TIFICATION OF LOST AND STOLEN BICYCLES AND PROVIDING
    A PENALTY FOR VIOLATION HEREOF

BE IT ORDAINED BY THE CITY COUNCIL OF THE CITY OF XYZ
    as follows:

Section 1. That each and every owner or person in charge
or control of a bicycle or bicycles, except dealers thereof,
within the corporate limits of the city of Xyz, shall, within
thirty (30) days from and after the passage of this ordinance, register said bicycles with the Chief of Police of the
City of Xyz, by making application for registration in writ-

The passion to legislate should be controlled by facts concerning what legislation does actually achieve. Sometimes a very simple set of rules may be fairly adequate. For example, on submarines and other ships with no medical officer the practice of medicine is reduced to two rules: "If you can see it, put iodine on it. If you can't see it, give a dose of salts." Comparable rules in the administration of

---

ing, upon blanks furnished by said Chief of Police, which application shall state the name and address of the owner or person in charge and control of such bicycle or bicycles and the make and kind of bicycle and the factory number thereof, and from whom same was purchased, and such other description and information relative thereto as may in the judgment of said Chief of Police be necessary and proper for the identification thereof, and thereupon the Chief of Police of the city of Xyz, upon the payment to him, for the use and benefit of the City of Xyz, by said applicant, of not more than fifty (50) cents, shall issue to such applicant an identification metal tag, having thereon in raised figures and letters the word Xyz and a serial number, which tag shall be immediately placed and securely attached by such owner or person in charge or control of such bicycle or bicycles, upon the front upright bar of said bicycle and at and just below the handle bars thereof, so that the same may be plainly seen, and which metal tag shall at all times remain on said bicycle and not be removed therefrom, and said Chief of Police of the City of Xyz, at the same time shall give to said owner or person in charge or control of such bicycle or bicycles an identification card to be carried at all times by the owner thereof when said bicycle is in use, having upon it the identification number assigned to the owner of such bicycle registered, and also stating the name and address of the owner and a brief description of such bicycle.

*Section 2.* The Chief of Police of the City of Xyz, shall be and is hereby required to carefully file and preserve said

justice might be: "Let any tip-top person do what he feels like doing. Let any thoroughly worthless and vicious person be sent to live with his kind in a penal colony. Let disputes between those of intermediate status be decided by flipping a coin or splitting the difference!" But even if these worked well they would not deny the value of the elaborate fabric of legal rules any more than the beneficence of the

---

applications set out in Section 1, and to keep a register of all bicycles for which said metal identification tags and cards are issued, which register shall contain the name of the owner or person in charge or control of such bicycle or bicycles, the make and factory number of the bicycle, and the number of the identification tag, and such other memoranda as may be, in the discretion of said Chief of Police, necessary and proper for the carrying out of the purpose of this ordinance.

*Section 3.* Whenever any person, other than a dealer thereof, sells, trades or transfers any bicycle, he shall endorse upon said identification card a written transfer of the same, naming the person and address to whom the same is transferred, and such transferee shall immediately notify the Chief of Police of such transfer to him, and said Chief of Police shall issue a new identification card in the name of such transferee, which identification card shall bear the original number of the metal identification tag and the number of the original card, and enter upon his register, provided for in Section 2, the name and address of the transferee and purchaser thereof.

*Section 4.* In the event the said metal identification tag or identification card provided for by this ordinance be lost or stolen or removed from such bicycle, the owner or person in charge or control of such bicycle shall immediately notify the Chief of Police of the City of Xyz, of the loss of same, and the Chief of Police of Xyz, shall, when such owner or person in charge or control of such bicycle, makes proper affidavit of the loss of said metal tag or said card, stating

iodine and/or salts practice denies the value of medical science. Moreover the law has not increased in complexity more than life in general has; and every added complexity of life may well require a new custom and a new rule to recommend and enforce the custom.

My personal opinion is that the law may wisely be trusted to improve itself. It did happen once that

---

the facts of said loss as nearly as possible, issue to said owner or person in charge or control of such bicycle, upon payment to the Chief of Police, for the use and benefit of the City of Xyz, of not more than fifty (50) cents, a new identification tag or card or both as the case may be, for such bicycle.

*Section 5.* It is hereby expressly declared to be the duty of each and every owner and person in charge or control of any bicycle to immediately notify the Chief of Police of the City of Xyz, of the loss by theft or otherwise of such bicycle.

*Section 6.* It shall be the duty of every person, firm or corporation dealing in bicycles in the City of Xyz, either as a business or as an occasional buyer and seller of the same, to keep, in a well-bound book, at his place of business, a record of all bicycles bought and sold and rented by him, giving an accurate description of such bicycle and from whom received, together with his address and the factory number thereof and serial number thereof, if any, to whom sold and rented, giving their names and addresses and the number of the identification tag and identification card, if any, together with the date of such transactions, in a plain and legible handwriting, which book shall at all times be open to the inspection of the Chief of Police of the City of Xyz, or any officer designated by said Chief of Police to perform said duty.

*Section 7.* It is hereby declared to be unlawful, from and after thirty (30) days after the passage and approval and going into effect of this ordinance, for any person, acting either for himself or any other person, to change the factory

a great lawyer who was also a psychologist, Jeremy Bentham, recommended changes which were later made to the great advantage of the law and human welfare. Perhaps it will happen again.

---

number on any bicycle and to remove or permit such identification metal tag to be removed from the same, or to use any bicycle without the same being registered as herein provided for and having had issued to him, and placed upon the bicycle, the metal identification tag, or to use any bicycle without the same has thereon displayed, in the place provided for in Section 1 hereof, the metal identification tag, or to fail or refuse to make said application and register the same.

*Section 8.* The provisions of this ordinance are mandatory and any failure or neglect or refusal or violation of the same is hereby declared a misdemeanor, punishable upon conviction by the Corporation Court of the City of Xyz, by fine in any sum not to exceed Fifty ($50.00) Dollars and not less than One ($1.00) Dollar.

*Section 9.* Whereas there are a great number of bicycles in use in the City of Xyz, and there is daily a great loss of bicycles by owners thereof by theft and otherwise and there is no sufficient record or means of identifying said lost and stolen bicycles and there is no ordinance providing for a registration of the same so that same can be properly identified and recovered, which creates a public emergency justifying a suspension of the charter ruling requiring that all ordinances be read at two regular meetings of the City Council, the said charter rule is hereby suspended by the consent of the Mayor and the unanimous vote of all Aldermen present and this ordinance shall take effect and be in force from and after its passage and publication.

It would surely have been more effective, and also cheaper, for this city to have provided bicycle locks for all bicycles.

## VIII

## THE PSYCHOLOGY OF PUNISHMENT

As GOVERNMENTS ARE and have been, coercion is essential; and punishment for breaking the law and for disobeying a ruler's commands is the commonest means of coercion. Punishment has been widely used not only by governments, but also by the home, the school, the church, and other human institutions.

The orthodox doctrine of government, and also the doctrine of common sense, has been that punishments of a tendency weaken it in ways comparable to the ways in which rewards strengthen it. Students of penology have noted certain failures of punishments to reform law-breakers or prevent crime, and have suggested that the inevitableness of a punishment is more effective than its severity. The general increase of humane feelings and customs during the last hundred years has been accompanied by a lessening in both the frequency and the magnitude of bodily punishments. But punishment is still relied on as the force behind the law — of nation, state, city, school, church, family, or playground. The orthodox doctrine to which psychologists have given their silent assent is still that punishment will weaken tendencies as much and as surely as rewards will strengthen them. The assent of psychologists has not always been silent. Yerkes suggested, in connection with his multiple-choice experiments, that animals might learn better if motivated by punishment, which up till then had been little used in psychological experiments, and he used solitary confinement as a punishment. Warden and Aylesworth expected that punishing the wrong choices in addition to rewarding the right would favor learning, and carried out experiments to measure its influence. So also did Kuo. As was suggested in an earlier lecture, there are grave defects in this orthodox doctrine.

A dozen years ago, from 1928 to 1931, I made many experiments in multiple-choice learning with human subjects. These experiments were designed to measure and compare the increase in probability of recurrence, upon recurrence of a situation, of a rewarded connection, with the decrease in probability of recurrence of a punished connection, all circumstances except the reward and the punishment being as nearly identical as possible.

What was my surprise to find that a connection made and punished was more likely to be made again than if it had not been made at all! All my later results confirmed the fact. Dr. Irving Lorge found the same.

I then spent many weary hours in analyzing the learning of the crows of Coburn and Yerkes, the pigs of Yerkes and Coburn, the canaries of Sadovinkova, and the monkeys of Yerkes.[1] The situation was pres-

[1] C. A. Coburn and R. M. Yerkes, "A study of the behavior of the crow Corvus Americanus (Audubon) by the multiple-

ence in a chamber and confrontation by a row of from three to nine compartments. The reward for entering a certain compartment was an open road to food and freedom. The punishment for entering any other compartment was confinement for thirty seconds, with no food. The records showed little or no evidence of any weakening of the tendency to enter a given compartment as a consequence of having been punished for having done so. The learning by these animals could all be accounted for by the rewardings of their right choices, plus a tendency to try to run back out of wrong compartments before the entrance was blocked.

Kuo had thirteen rats put in a choice chamber repeatedly, where they could choose from four exits which we will call $c$, $e$, $l$, and $s$. Choice of $c$ was punished by confinement for twenty seconds; choice of $e$ was punished by an electric shock "strong enough to make the animal squeal every time and immediately jump back"; choice of $l$ was rewarded by food after a path of about twelve feet was traversed; choice of $s$ was rewarded by food after a short path of about a foot was traversed. Their individual histories for the

choice method," *Journal of Animal Behavior*, V, 75–114 (1915); R. M. Yerkes and C. A. Coburn, "A study of the behavior of the pig Sus scrofa by the multiple-choice method," *Journal of Animal Behavior*, V, 185–225 (1915); M. P. Sadovinkova, "A study of the behavior of birds by the multiple-choice method," *Journal of Comparative Psychology*, III, 249–282 (1923); R. M. Yerkes, "The mental life of monkeys and apes; a study of ideational bevahior," *Behavior Monographs*, vol. III, no. 12, pp. 1–145 (1916).

first twenty-four trials are shown below. Analysis of these and the later histories made it probable that the *e* connection was not weakened by the shock, but was supplanted by the *s* connection, or more rarely by the *l* connection.

RESPONSES OF 13 RATS IN SUCCESSIVE TRIALS WITH KUO'S MULTIPLE-CHOICE APPARATUS [2]

(c, e, l, *and* s *signify, respectively, entrances to the compartments where confinement, an electric shock, a long path to food, and a short path to food were the consequences.*)

| RAT | TRIAL | | | | | |
|---|---|---|---|---|---|---|
| | 1 2 3 4 | 5 6 7 8 | 9 10 11 12 | 13 14 15 16 | 17 18 19 20 | 21 22 23 24 |
| 1 | c l e s | e s e l | e s c l | e s s s | c e c e | l c s s |
| 2 | l e l e | s e e e | l l e c | c s c e | s e l l | e e l c |
| 3 | e s e s | e e c s | l e e l | c e s c | s s e s | s s l l |
| 4 | s c e l | c l e l | l l e l | l s c s | l l s l | l l c l |
| 5 | c e s c | s e l e | c s c l | s c c s | s l c l | s l c s |
| 6 | e c s e | s s e s | s c l l | e l l l | s s s s | s s s s |
| 7 | c e l c | e l l s | s l l l | l s l l | s s l l | c s s l |
| 8 | s c s e | s s s l | l l e c | l l e s | s s s s | s s s s |
| 9 | c l e l | e s l l | e l s s | s s s s | s s s s | s s s s |
| 10 | l e s c | s s l l | l l l l | l l c l | l l l l | l l l l |
| 11 | s c s l | e l l l | s l s s | s c l s | l l s l | l s s l |
| 12 | s e l l | c l e c | l l l l | l l l l | c l l l | l l l l |
| 13 | l e l s | c l e l | c e l s | s s s s | c s c s | s l c l |

I then proceeded to measure the effect, or absence of effect, of punishment upon animals by more extensive and crucial experiments. With the assistance of Dr. Robert Thorndike, I got the facts for each of

[2] Z. Y. Kuo, "The nature of unsuccessful acts, and their order of elimination in animal learning," *Journal of Comparative Psychology*, II, 8 (1922). Quoted by permission of the publishers, The Williams and Wilkins Company, Baltimore.

sixty-four chicks in twenty, or sometimes thirty, experiences with each of six different chambers with three exit compartments, entrance to one of the three being rewarded whereas entrance or attempted entrance to either of the others was punished. There were nearly ten thousand recorded observations of the chicks' behavior in their successive experiences. The reward was always exit to freedom, food, and the company of other chicks. The punishment was either confinement for thirty seconds in the entered compartment, or simply being thwarted in the effort to escape from the chamber.

In these experiments also, reward strengthened, but punishment did not weaken, the tendencies to which it was attached. A better prophecy is had by reckoning the influence of a punished occurrence upon the probability of recurrence as zero or slightly positive than by giving it any negative influence.

It had become certain, at least to me, that punishment was not a dynamic opposite of reward. It did not arouse an inhibiting reaction comparable to the confirming reaction. If a reward, such as the announcement "Right" or such announcement plus a money payment, is attached to a mental tendency the tendency is directly strengthened thereby; but of a punishment, such as the announcement "Wrong" or such announcement plus a sharp electric shock, is attached to a mental tendency all else being equal the tendency is not weakened thereby. So experiments with human subjects were devised to give punishment special advantages. In these experiments, conducted by Dr. J. V. Waits, the situation was choice among five responses, namely, hitting five keys on a modified typewriter, but at each appearance of the situation the subject kept on responding until he hit the right key. That is, he would see and hit a key and get a signal telling whether his response was right or wrong. If it was wrong he would hit again. If this second hit was wrong, he would hit still again, and so on until he hit the right key, when a new situation would appear and he would respond to it. He thus responded to each of forty pictures (or words) until he attained the right connection. The forty pictures (or words) were then presented again and he again chose for each until he attained the right connection. And so on for five rounds of the series of forty.[3]

[3] A more detailed description of the apparatus and procedure is given by Dr. Waits as follows:

"A mechanical device was designed and constructed to present the stimulus situations, as well as to administer the reward or punishment immediately after the response. A modified typewriter was used as the responding mechanism since it could be adapted to serve the double purpose of allowing a multiple choice and also of recording the choice.

"A learning situation was presented to which the subject had choice among five responses. One of these responses was arbitrarily designated as right and the others as wrong. The situation was a stimulus word or nonsense symbol with which the subject was to learn to associate one of the five typewriter keys, lettered F, G, H, J, or K. The stimulus was exposed in a small aperture at eye level before the subject. He indicated his choice of letter by striking one of the five keys on the typewriter, all other keys (than the five) having been removed from the machine. His choice was recorded by his stroke, and

In all the earlier experiments with human subjects the situation vanished after one response to it, and did not appear again for a considerable time, but in these the situation remained until a successful response closed the episode. In ordinary life both sorts of experience occur. In playing tennis, for example, the situation of a certain ball coming in a certain way vanishes after one response, not to recur for minutes or hours or days. In translating a passage a word remains while one after another meaning is tried until a satisfying one is found, when the person proceeds to another word. The second sort guarantees to punishment in the case of intelligent persons at least so much potency as comes from then and there changing from the punished connection to some other.

---

by means of a series of electrical connections he was immediately rewarded if his choice were the one designated as right, or punished if it were one designated as wrong. In the instructions, each subject was told that he would receive a reward of one-tenth of a cent for each right and that he would receive a punishment of a slight electric shock and lose one-tenth of a cent for each wrong response. He received information of a right response from the ringing of a small bell.

"When a right key was struck and the reward given, immediately a new situation appeared in the aperture. When a wrong key was struck and the punishment administered, the situation was retained so that the subject could make another choice. In this way a second, third, fourth, or fifth choice was allowed. That is, the situation remained in view of the subject until he responded with the choice arbitrarily designated as right for that situation, though after each choice the subject was either punished or rewarded according to whether the choice made was wrong or right. If the subject did not discover the correct response until he had tried all five keys, he

In spite of its specially favorable opportunities punishment did not permanently weaken the connections to which it was attached in these experiments. Punishment did cause the subject to avoid repeating the connection at once. That is, if he hit a wrong key he shifted to another. But when, *after thirty-nine other situations had been presented,* the situation recurred, the punishment did no good. This can be shown in several ways. One is to compute the probability of a recurrence by chance and compare the actual recurrence with it. A connection punished in trial 1 appears in trial 2 *oftener* than it would by chance. Another is to compare experiences in which

---

received a punishment after each of his first four responses, and a reward after the fifth response. As soon as the correct response to one stimulus situation was made, a new one appeared, and so on until forty stimulus situations had been presented. . . .

"When the correct response for the fortieth stimulus situation had been made the series began again, that is, the first stimulus reappeared ànd a second trial on all forty items was given. Five trials for each set of forty stimuli were administered to each subject. . . .

"The set-up might be compared to a maze with forty points of choice, at each of which were five options, one of which would lead to a reward, and the other four would lead to punishment. It is similar to the maze experiment in that the subject must dsicover the correct response for each point of choice before progressing to the next one; and the stimulus situation is retained until the correct choice is made. It differs from the maze in that the reward is given after each right choice and not at the completion of the whole maze."

(J. V. Waits, "The Law of Effect in the Retained Situation," Archives of Psychology, No. 208, p. 18 f. 1937. Quoted by permission.)

four, three, two, one, and no connections were punished before the right connection was made and rewarded. For the influence of the experience of the first round or trial upon the behavior in the second round the facts were as follows:

Experience in Trial 1

| | Percentage of cases in Trial 2 in which the first response made was right |
|---|---|
| 4 punished connections followed by 1 rewarded connection | 25 |
| 3 punished connections followed by 1 rewarded connection | 32 |
| 2 punished connections followed by 1 rewarded connection | 31 |
| 1 punished connection followed by 1 rewarded connection | 35 |
| 0 punished connections followed by 1 rewarded connection | 57 |

Call the right connection S→C and the wrong connections S→$X_1$, S→$X_2$, S→$X_3$, S→$X_4$. The person learns faster from the reward of S→C alone than from the reward of S→C plus the punishment of any or all of S→$X_1$, S→$X_2$, etc. This is true also for the influence of the experiences of Trial 2, Trial 3, and Trial 4. The subjects in the experiment make fewer and fewer wrong connections, but this is entirely due to the strengthening of rewarded connections, which then displace the punished.

If, as now seems certain, punishment is not the psychological opposite of reward, and has no necessary direct weakening influence upon tendencies to which it is attached, what influence does it have? What can it do? Its various forms have whatever influence the genes and the experience of life have given them. Reaching forth and touching an object, if punished by a burn or prick, may cause withdrawal by virtue of the genes. The relief attached to withdrawal from that object may arouse a confirming reaction of the tendency to withdraw which indirectly weakens the reaching tendency. Wearing a coat on a summer day, if punished by heat and sweat, may cause one to take the coat off by virtue of the experiences of life. The relief attached to the coatless condition may arouse a confirming reaction that weakens the tendency to put on a coat on a summer day.

Punishments can do what they are actually observed to do. It is unsafe to expect more from them. Certain punishments arouse fears of certain persons, things, places, events, etc., and thus cause whatever the fear causes. Certain punishments arouse shame, and indirectly cause whatever the shame causes. Fear and shame associated with a connection may reduce its probability of occurrence greatly. Being punished in one's movement forward may make one turn and go back. Being punished at a certain spot may make one run away from that spot. All punishments give information and some give it very impressively. A man, not an idiot, who is tried, convicted, and put in prison for stealing an automobile can hardly forget that if he is caught stealing an automobile he will be put in prison. Anyone's experiences of punishment, personal by suffering it in certain circumstances and vicarious by witnessing, hearing about, or reading about the punishment of others, operate in his thought and conduct in the same way as, but often more emphatically than, his experiences of the uses of foods and drinks, the purchasing power of money, the services of a doctor, or priest, or any other feature of life.

Finally a punishment co-acting with a reward may neutralize the latter and prevent it from arousing a confirming reaction. If a certain indulgence, say drinking a glass of beer, is accompanied by a certain punishment, say paying a nickel therefor, the habit may in a certain man be stabilized at three beers a day, whereas if he could get beer for nothing he would rapidly change to drinking a dozen a day. The hedonic calculus does operate in man, though not in the manner or to the extent that Bentham thought.

Whatever be the details of their operation, it is highly probable that punishments do their best service when they somehow cause the person to do what is right and to receive a confirming reaction for so doing. In those experiments with animals in which punishment does aid learning (for example, in the experiments of Warden and Aylesworth), there is a choice between two alleys, and the animal punished in one often runs back out and into the other, for doing which he is rewarded. Unless punishing the wrong somehow causes confirmation of the right, we may be suspicious of its efficacy. It may, as in our experiments, do more harm by occurring than good by being punished. The best preventives of crimes and follies are the operation and confirmation of good and prudent habits. Punishments may have undesirable by-products. Results attained by the arousal of fears may be costly because fears tend to lower the person's activity and enterprise. They also may act as wounds to the mind, festering in its depths and causing neuroses of one sort or another. They also too easily attach themselves not to the thing or act that deserves to be feared and avoided, but to some less relevant associate of it, as when punishment leaves a habit fully active but evokes measures to prevent its detection.

A punishment may cause hate and direct it against the punisher. The more just the punishment, the more subversive of civilization and morality such hates are. There is usually a net loss when punishment cures a child of a bad habit at the cost of causing him to hate his father, or when it cures a man of a criminal tendency at the cost of causing him to hate society. Some psychiatrists think that hate directed toward the punisher is a very common result of punishment. Karl Menninger, for example, considers the following chant which a four-year-old composed and used every day in his bath as a genuine hymn of hate toward those in authority over him:

He will just do nothing at all,
He will just sit there in the noonday sun.
And when they speak to him, he will not answer them,
Because he does not care to.
He will stick them with spears and put them in the
    garbage.

When they tell him to eat his dinner, he will just laugh
    at them,
And he will not take his nap, because he does not care to.
He will not talk to them, he will not say nothing,
He will just sit there in the noonday sun.
He will go away and play with the Panda.
He will not speak to nobody because he doesn't have to.
And when they come to look for him they will not find
    him,
Because he will not be there.
He will put spikes in their eyes and put them in the
    garbage,
And put the cover on.
He will not go out in the fresh air or eat his vegetables
Or make wee-wee for them, and he will get thin as a
    marble.
He will not do nothing at all.
He will just sit there in the noonday sun.[4]

We may prefer to enjoy this as a literary master-
piece and congratulate the parents of so gifted a
four-year-old, rather than to use it as a measure of
childhood's hatred of coercion and coercers. And in
general we may hope that a vast amount of punishment is accepted as a part of the order of nature without hatred of parent, teacher, policeman, judge, or
anybody else. But we must all admit that punishment has to its discredit a substantial volume of pernicious hate.

The reformative and preventive action of punishments by way of fear, shame, and self-interest needs

[4] From *The New Yorker*, July 1, 1939, quoted by Menninger on p. 20, of *Love against Hate*, 1942. Copyrighted.
Reprinted by permission of *The New Yorker*.

extensive study to measure what it does accomplish, and intensive analysis to learn how it accomplishes it. The facts about their reformative and preventive action upon convicted offenders are not encouraging. Indeed it seems likely that if a thousand such were separated into two random halves, one of which was left unpunished, the future careers of the two groups would not differ greatly. But perhaps there are beneficial effects upon non-offenders, who may have been prevented from breaking the law. It is not fair to measure the effects of punishments by their effects upon law-breakers only.

The approved practices in institutions which have notable records of improving boys and girls, and especially of curing bad habits, seem to make very little use of punishments. If, for example, you will examine the case histories reported in *Children Astray* by Drucker and Hexter, you will find in the descriptions of what the orphanage did many instances of reward by praise and other forms of approval, by privileges, and by money and other gifts, but hardly any instances of punishment, unless the necessary capture and return to the institution of a child who runs away is counted as a punishment. The essentials of the treatment are described by Dr. Richard Cabot in his introduction to the book as "Sympathetic understanding . . . the discovery and cultivation of the child's strong points, the creative power of affection (when it can be developed), the dynamic of an ambition to 'be somebody' and accomplish something, the influence of a Big Brother or a Big Sister, the discipline of regular school work, manual work, scouting, and pet animals." [5] In this the only suggestion of punishment is its possibility as a part of "the discipline of regular school work."

Dr. Ella Woodyard and I have studied the effect of rewards and punishments upon a group of persons high in ability and morality, namely persons whose biographies have been written. Dr. Woodyard searched through 1068 English and American biographies, and found 191 reported instances of a reward or a punishment. In the case of 88 of these the biography included some testimony concerning the effect of the reward or punishment. The rewards were said to have been beneficial in 29 cases out of 30; the punishments in 17 cases out of 58. Crudely the rewards are thus reported as doing 29 times as much good as harm; and the punishments as doing 2½ times as much harm as good. I do not think that the biographers or those from whom they got their material were prejudiced against punishment. On the contrary, most of them were written before the days of soft pedagogy, when "Spare the rod and spoil the child" was almost unquestioned, when the Prince Consort was pinched for a failure in grammar, and flogging was an everyday occurrence in the most aristocratic schools.

There are now many homes and schools in which there is practically no punishment other than by disapproval and occasional deprivations, and in which

[5] Richard C. Cabot, Introduction to *Children Astray* by Saul Drucker and Maurice Beck Hexter, 1923, p. xxii.

threats of punishment are almost equally rare. The children in such homes turn out very well. Perhaps they would turn out well under any régime, but they prove at least that home and school punishments are not indispensable, and that their efficacy has been over-rated in ancient lore and customs.

Until the whole matter of punishment by governments has been studied adequately, it seems prudent to regard it as an unreliable, and in some ways a dangerous, social tool, and to retain it, not so much because of any intrinsic merits, as because it may prevent something much worse. Punishments by government may be valuable as a substitute for punishments by individuals which would be less effective, as well as less equitable, and more damaging to the punishers. This applies also to coercion other than by punishment. Coercion by governments may include follies and injustices, and still be much preferable to coercion by those individuals who happen to have power to coerce or a talent for acquiring it. Nobody is entirely fit to rule his fellow-men, but somebody must. No set of rules yet devised is perfect, but even a very faulty set is better than none. No set of punishments will guarantee obedience to the rules, but those selected by experts and used by courts will work better than private vengeance. The coercion of human individuals is in many respects a profitless and deplorable business, but a recognized, public, predictable coercion under the law is an insurance against a chaos of stupid, fanatical and vicious punishment of the weak by the powerful.

These statements are probably justified by both psychology and history, and fit to use as axioms. But they are surely no excuse for failure to study governments, laws, and punishments scientifically, or for neglect of ways and means to improve them.

Psychology recommends that much more care be taken to attach the confirming reaction (see Chapter II) to desirable tendencies. Strengthening the habits whereby a person earns an honest living seems likely to be a more fruitful enterprise for government than punishing theft, forgery, and the like. Strengthening the habits of healthful recreation, fair play, mutual aid, and kindliness seems likely to be more fruitful than punishing crimes of violence. Playgrounds seem more promising investments than prisons; and perhaps public work-shops where any boy or girl who wanted to earn money would be paid as much as his services were worth would also be a good social investment. Restriction of child-labor and the extension of the years of compulsory school attendance are two great achievements of modern good will toward the young. We may well be proud of them. But they involve some dangers when they deprive boys and girls of the rewards that come from productive labor. Should we not somehow protect childhood and youth from the greed of cruel or ignorant parents and from ruthless exploitation by cruel or incompetent employers without denying them the chance to earn and spend and save?

Psychology recommends fuller and more ingenious uses of public reward by citations, medals, and other decorations, honor rolls, and other marks of community approval. It would recommend them more emphatically except for one defect — that they usually operate only on the top levels of ability and character. Perhaps this defect is remediable. It characterized the rewards of the older schools but has been remedied in many today. There are classrooms where every pupil is stimulated to do something well and is rewarded for some excellence. This may be done so skilfully that the boy who is praised for his competence in cleaning the blackboard is as much encouraged in doing his best as the girl who leads the class in scholarship. Perhaps even some very simple schemes would work. Suppose that the rulers of a community drew up a list each year of all those who have deserved well of the community, and drew by chance one name per fifty from that list for public mention and reward. The millions of worthy citizens who now receive no encouragement in well-doing from the government or the public would have one chance in fifty each year, and could at least live in hope. This will seem childish to many of you — and it is childish. But the American citizen is a mixture of childishness and sophistication, and it may be wise for government to consider both aspects of him.

Things being as they are in the world today, you may expect me to say something about the punishment of nation by nation, and the punishment of groups of nations by groups of nations.

A nation is not a person and it is unsafe to extend psychological conclusions from persons to nations.

But there is no reason to expect our conclusions about rewards and punishments to be reversed in the case of nations. The wise policy for those responsible for the welfare of the world is then presumably to reward each and every nation when it keeps the peace, obeys international law, does not breed disease or vice, advances science and the fine and useful arts, and otherwise contributes to the welfare of the world. Little in either psychology or history leads one to expect much good from punishing a nation, even supposing that the punishments are all perfectly just. The case of a nation seems even less promising than that of a person, because the influence through shame, strong in persons, is very weak in nations. Even the best nation is rarely ashamed of its sins.

There remain the consequences through fear and hate. Experts in history and social psychology do not yet know how far salutary consequences of national fear outweigh its depressive influence and its tendency to resort to futile or harmful expedients to gain future security. We may hope that the verdicts of an international court would cause fears at least as salutary as those caused by floods or epidemics. But we must consider the possibility that a sinning nation punished justly for a sin would continue its sin in secret if it could. National hate toward the agencies of the just punishment there almost certainly would be, until the government, press, and populace of a nation acquire a national modesty and objectivity that no nation has ever yet possessed.

If punishments for breaking international law administered by an international court cannot be expected to do much good, they would still be infinitely superior to punishments of one another by individual nations. The latter are of negative value, definitely pernicious. They put the small at the mercy of the great, the weak at the mercy of the strong, and the peaceful at the mercy of the belligerent. They lack even the slight protections which the genes provide for individual men, in the form of certain natural checks on brutality, as by kindliness and by the tendency of a human group to treat a brutal individual as a wild animal. A weak nation cannot take refuge in flight. It cannot transfer or hide its property. When each individual takes the law into his own hands, the innocent have some advantage over the guilty, if both are equally weak. The innocent has a better conscience and has greater probability of help from society. But when each nation takes the law into its own hands, a powerful nation can always find excuses for punishing whatever weak nation it chooses, no matter how innocent a bystander that nation may be.

International coöperation to remedy international injustices, to ensure the weak equal rights with the strong, and to prevent lawless strife, by international law, international courts, and international police, is then estimable. But international coöperation to prevent national crimes by directing the energies of nations into desirable activities and rewarding these activities is better.

## IX

## THE PSYCHOLOGY OF WELFARE: THE
## WELFARE OF INDIVIDUALS

THERE ARE TWO oddly contrasted characteristics of this century, the magnitude of its wars, and the wide acceptance of the gospel of welfare in this life by its intellectual and moral leaders. The welfare of living men has been the conscious goal of professionals like Beatrice and Sidney Webb and amateurs like Andrew Carnegie. Philanthropy, or "social work" as its professors prefer to call it, has become a recognized profession with its schools and degrees; and the benevolence of donors has shifted from conventional charities and uplifts, preparation for heaven, and protection against hell to deliberate rational work for mundane welfare.

I have examined the descriptions of what constitutes welfare without finding anything adequate, or even anything that attempts to be adequate. Many moralists and reformers and social workers have, properly enough, been so busy with advocating and making particular gains for welfare that they have not bothered to consider it as a whole. Some have been so devoted to sweeping doctrines that they have not bothered to consider the concrete facts.

We obviously need a set of specifications showing the constituents of welfare, and I present a set which is the best that I can at present offer.

A BILL OF SPECIFICATIONS OF A GOOD LIFE FOR MAN

1. Maintenance of the inner causes of the joy of living at or above their present average.

2. Food when hungry, and drink when thirsty.

3. A diet that is physiologically adequate.

4. Protection against pain-causing animals.

5. Protection against disease-causing organisms, poisons, and other causes of disease.

6. Protection or insurance against accidents and disasters, such as floods, earthquakes, wars, for which the person in question is not responsible.

7. Protection against extreme shocks, fear, and strains.

8. Some room or place where he can rest undisturbed, protected from the elements and from bad or uncongenial men.

9. Enjoyable bodily activity, especially when young.

10. Enjoyable mental activity, including esthetic pleasures.

11. Opportunity for human society.

12. Opportunity for courtship, love, and life with one's mate.

13. Opportunity to care for children and to be kind to human beings and animals.

14. The approval of one's community, or at least the absence of scorn or contempt.

15. The approval of one's self, self-respect, the absence of shame and remorse.

16. Opportunity to have friends and affection, if deserving of them.

17. Opportunity to be a friend and give affection.

18a. Opportunity to exercise power over some persons, animals, things, or ideas, making them do one's will.

18b. Opportunity to serve a worthy master.

19. Membership in organized groups, and the right to participate in activities or ceremonies which are (or at least are thought to be) important.

20. Opportunity to compete with one's peers winning in about 50 per cent of the trials.

21. Opportunity to compete with one's own past record, and, if deserving, to have the pleasures of achievement and success.

22. Occasional opportunities for adventure, risk, and danger.

23. Something to be angry at and attack.

24. Protection by society (via customs, laws, and government) in what is regarded by the existing moral code as a good life.

25. Freedom to discover and publish verifiable truth.

26. Enjoyment of the happiness of others.

I suggest that sometime at your leisure each of you should improve the list until it satisfies you. Let each of you think of himself as a trustee for mankind faced with the task of making a rough bill of specifications to show what welfare really is and to be a guide for the labors of the able and good in the service of man. Bear in mind that you should include the satisfactions possible for men today without imperiling the welfare of future men. Bear in mind that certain human wants conflict with others, and that you should plan for a reasonable compromise in such cases. You will find the experience instructive. I shall be very glad to receive copies of your amendments, as an aid to my future thinking.

My list is doubtless fallible, but it has the merits of being impartial, definite, and adapted to human nature, and of being more attainable and maintainable than many prescriptions for welfare are. I will comment upon some of its items.

The inclusion of item 1 (Maintenance of the inner causes of the joy of living at or above their present average) is a consequence of certain studies of human likes and dislikes which I made a few years ago with the help of many friends. The first records obtained were from an Interest Sheet like that shown below.[1]

### INTEREST SHEET

Please consider the activities listed below from the point of view of your interest in them at age 20–29. Enter a number from +5 to −5 for your degree of like or dislike for each of these activities at age twenty to twenty-nine. The meanings of the numbers from −5 to +5 are to be as follows:

−5  Extremely unpleasant; comparable to having a dentist work on my teeth, to a bad headache, or to being made a fool of in public.

−4  Very unpleasant, but not quite as bad as −5.

−3  If you are in doubt whether to rate your dislike −4 or −2, call it −3.

−2  Would never do it except from duty or as a means to some desired end.

−1  Mildly disliked rather than liked.

 0  Indifference; neither liked nor disliked.

+1  Mildly liked.

+2  Would do without hesitation if I had the chance, and if nothing more interesting was available.

+3  If you are in doubt whether to rate your liking +2 or +4, call it +3.

+4  Very enjoyable, but not quite so much so as +5.

+5  As much liked as almost anything I can think of.

[1] This sheet was accompanied by explanatory notes.

Do the same for ages 30 to 39, 40 to 49, and 50 to 59.

| | At age 20–29 | At age 30–39 | At age 40–49 | At age 50–59 |
|---|---|---|---|---|
| 1. Reading fiction | ........ | ........ | ........ | ........ |
| 2. Reading non-fiction (except newspapers) | ........ | ........ | ........ | |
| 3. Reading the newspaper | ........ | ........ | ........ | ........ |
| 4. Outdoor sports, not competitive (hunting, fishing, swimming, hiking, etc.) | ........ | ........ | ........ | ...... |
| 5. Outdoor competitive games | ........ | ........,,, | ........ | |
| 6. Sedentary games (cards, chess) | ........ | ........ | ........ | ........ |
| 7. Dancing | ........ | ........ | ........ | ........ |
| 8. Playing a musical instrument | ........ | ........ | ........ | ........ |
| 9. Listening to music | ........ | ........ | ........ | ........ |
| 10. Theatre or movies | ........ | ........ | ........ | ........ |
| 11. My regular job | ........ | ........ | ........ | ........ |
| 12. Politics | ........ | ........ | ........ | ........ |
| 13. Welfare work (in community organizations, the church, etc.) | ........ | ........ | ........ | ........ |
| 14. Talking with old friends | ........ | ........ | ........ | ........ |
| 15. Making new acquaintances | ........ | ........ | ........ | ........ |
| 16. Traveling and seeing new places | ........ | ........ | ........ | ........ |
| 17. Sheer idleness, doing nothing, thinking of nothing | ........ | ........ | ........ | ........ |

There was a wide range of difference among individuals in what I call *gen-like*, a tendency to like many things, and much. For example, consider individual X in whom gen-like is strong and individual Y in whom gen-like is weak. X has +5 at all four age periods (20–29, 30–39, 40–49, and 50–59) for all of the sixteen items except reading fiction, for which his average is $-2$, sedentary games, for which his average is 0, and dancing, for which his average is 0. His average is $+4.2$. X does like very much all the activities which he rates $+5$. He probably would have liked playing cards and dancing very much, except for the fact that he was a Methodist minister! His ratings do measure him. Y averages $+0.4$. Y does not get keen enjoyment out of anything except working with tools and machinery. His ratings do measure him.

In later studies of likes and dislikes covering 587 items, the existence and importance of *gen-like* was confirmed. There are probably some fortunate people who like getting up out of bed, shaving and dressing, reading their mail and answering it, seeing callers, attending weddings, attending funerals, arguing, fighting, persuading, giving lectures, and listening to lectures — who enjoy sermons, Sunday School, opera, theatre, movies, night-clubs, ball games, elections, committee reports, gardening, house-cleaning, embroidery, knitting, darning, patching, dishwashing, feeding the cows, feeding the pigs, and feeding the furnace. Think what the gain in welfare would be if all men could be inoculated with as much gen-like as these have. If I were thirty-eight instead of sixty-eight, I would try to find the causes, hereditary and environmental, of gen-like, and ways and means of increasing it in men.

Item 12 (Opportunity for courtship, love, and life with one's mate) is not intended to require that all adults be paired off in holy monogamic bonds. Nor are any of the other items to be interpreted as an identical provision for all persons, regardless of the individual natures which differentiate them. Some persons will need more of Item 9 (Enjoyable bodily activity) and less of Item 10 (Enjoyable mental activity) than others. The amount of Item 11 (Opportunity for human society) will be at least five times as much for some as for others. And similarly for other items. Men, women, children, adults, geniuses, idiots, thinkers, artists, and executives will take unequally from this list of opportunities.

Item 14 (The approval of one's community) and Item 15 (The approval of one's self) concern important wants which many Utopias and planned societies neglect. The craving for the approval of one's social community deserves to be ranked with the primary motives concerned with food, sex, and safety. There is, first of all, a general sensitiveness to the diffuse approval of the world as it filters through to all communities. And this is of great importance. Each locality and social group has also its special public opinion. Each person has a social community peculiar to him. The opinion of Cedar Street that John Smith the barber has done very well counts more to John Smith than the opinion of all polite literature that the barber's is a rather demeaning trade. The man whose abilities qualify him to be an unskilled laborer or machine hand usually has been born and bred in a group who do not in the least scorn him because he is an unskilled laborer. By them he is never made to feel a failure because he is not a professional man or expert tradesman. He is esteemed within his group as the tradesman is within his. Similarly a successful plumber usually feels no more degradation at not being a sanitary engineer than the average doctor feels at not being a Pasteur or a Lister. A plumber lives in a plumber's world. The prize-fighter cares as little for the economist's scorn of his intellect or the moralist's scorn of his trade as they care for the prize-fighter's scorn of their puny blows — probably less. The prize-fighter lives in a prize-fighter's world. Self-approval is even more necessary than the approval of others. Decent, healthy-minded, sensible people get it by realizing their abilities and opportunities, or their lacks in these respects, and using a reasonable amount of optimism. But even they are tempted to get it at the price of fallacious excuses and delusions.

Except for a very few darlings of fortune all of us are inferior to many in some respects. We are less intelligent, or less popular, or less skillful, with less wealth or power or public esteem, too thin, too fat, or too homely, lacking in magnetism, charm, or "it." But it is unpleasant to think so, and one is tempted to build up an inner private view of himself which he can contemplate enjoyably and approve heartily. Anything that would mar this inner image is then re-pelled or ejected from the mind, or neutralized by some contrary mental force. We are poor in this world's goods, because we have been ground under the iron heel of capital! We are not liked because we are misunderstood, or are of too fine a nature for the common herd! We are miserable sinners, but

God has chosen us and set us as jewels in his crown!

A wise philanthropy and skillful human engineering will enable a man to live happily with himself without debauching himself by fantasies and delusions.

Items 16 and 17 (Opportunity to have affection and to give affection) may call attention to the fact that over two thirds of our items relate to the soul rather than the body, and require personal and social rather than material provisions. They may also emphasize the fact that many of our items cost almost nothing save good personal qualities in men and women themselves.

Item 23 (Something to be angry at and attack) and item 25 (Freedom to discover and publish verifiable truth) may remind us that human wants range from those that are entirely good in the sense that their satisfaction in one man lessens no satisfaction of any other man to those that are almost entirely bad in the sense that the satisfaction of the want in one person thwarts or denies wants of other men and other and better wants of the man himself.

Among the wants that are entirely good are some which are superlatively good because their satisfaction in any one person actually adds to the sum of satisfactions of all men. Items 25 and 26 of our list are superlatively good in this sense.

Items 19, 20, and 21 are illustrations of a certain humble concreteness in our list. I offer no apology for this. On the contrary it seems better than grand generalities. Indeed I have intentionally avoided such items as liberty, equality, fraternity, socialization, and religion. We are in danger of not knowing what we mean by them. Their fruits for welfare are, I think, included in the list.

May I repeat my suggestion that you amend and extend this list into one that seems reasonable to you, and then use that in judging the merits of proposals for human betterments.

It is clear that the causation of welfare lies largely within men's brains or minds. It is by our brains that we control and modify the environment (physical, biological, and social) in the interest of welfare, so far as we do control it. It is by our brains that we evade it or adapt ourselves to it, where we cannot modify it.

It is clear that some individuals, by ability or goodness or both, make large contributions to welfare, and that others, by weakness, folly, vice, ill-will, or various combinations of these, reduce welfare. If enough facts were known, each person of a generation could be assigned his place on a scale running from the greatest benefactors to the greatest malefactors. If certain additional facts were known, these ratings could be corrected for the influence of circumstances, making them purer measures of positive and negative service to welfare according to opportunity. The scale would still range from Madame Curie and higher down to some who tormented their pets, robbed their mothers, raped little girls, and never did anything of value to anybody but themselves. It is almost certain that between these extremes every gradation is found.

It is not yet clear just how much of the variation

in contribution to welfare is the result of variation in genes, but no impartial student can doubt that much of it is. It is largely a resultant of variations in physical and mental health, intellect and other abilities, and character; and the genes are potent in all of these. In the case of the million or so persons coming of age this year in the United States, about three fourths of the variation in abstract intelligence is attributable to the genes they were born with. I venture the estimate that at least half of the variation in health, character, and other abilities than intellect is attributable to the genes. Welfare then depends largely upon who is being born. There is a natural, and in certain respects estimable, tendency among both amateur and professional workers for welfare to minimize the influence of the genes and to overestimate the influence of housing, schooling, economic status, and other environmental aids to welfare. It is relatively easy to apply these means of relief and possible prevention, and to do so is in accord with the sort of kindliness one's original nature provides. It is hard to prevent stupid, incompetent, brutal, and diseased persons from being born and still harder to raise the birth-rate of contributors to welfare; and the procedures necessary do not gratify the natural impulses to relieve, comfort, and console.

For these and other reasons the great bulk of welfare work, possibly ninety-nine per cent of it, pays no heed to the genes. This is ill-advised but perhaps excusable. What is inexcusable is a bigoted antagonism toward any efforts to select better genes for survival. Furthermore, ignorance of biology and psychology is no longer a sufficient excuse for relieving the miseries of the present by means which will increase the miseries of future men. As an illustration of unreasonable antagonism we may take the objection of an eminent British reformer to restricting in any way the procreative activities of the feeble-minded, which he defended by the fact that one of his friends found the feeble-minded very satisfactory as tenders of pigs! Nothing short of an obsession against eugenics could have led this very brilliant mind to desire a society some of whose members were fit only to tend other men's pigs.

As an illustration of the neglect of the welfare of future men we may take the zeal of some governments, and even of some sociologists, for an indiscriminate increase in the birth rate. Surely the quality of a nation's population or of the world's population is far more important to welfare than its quantity. Surely a world of two billion men such as they now are would be much inferior to a world of the one billion of them rating highest on a scale of service to welfare. Surely we should by now have discarded Paley's principle that a numerical increase of population is the best way to increase welfare.[2]

[2] "The quantity of happiness in a given district, although it is possible it may be increased, the number of inhabitants remaining the same, is chiefly and most naturally affected by alteration of the numbers . . . consequently the decay of population is the greatest decay that a state can suffer; and the improvement of it the object which ought, in all countries, to be aimed at in preference to every other political purpose

The perpetuation and increase of "good" genes and gene combinations is probably more important for welfare than the reduction and elimination of "bad" ones. The good done by one Pasteur probably outweighs the harm done by ten thousand carriers of typhoid. One Edison's achievements will support hundreds of thousands of unemployables for a lifetime. We could endure a horde of idiots if that would give us three intellects equal to Plato, Newton and Darwin. Moreover, a good gene lost is lost forever or until some new mutation recreates it; but a bad gene is more or less at our mercy, to be annihilated more or less easily when we so desire.

You may all admit that good genes and good combinations of genes are a most precious natural resource for welfare, but object that ways and means of conserving them are not "practical." This usually means that the ways and means the objector has in mind are not in accord with present customs. That is largely true; and sociology and psychology could perform a great service by discovering just where the conflicts reside, and seeking suitable causes to change the customs or to find ways of perpetuating good genes that would not conflict with them. I am confident that if even a few first-rate intellects spent even a few years on the problems substantial progress would be made.

A subtler objection to the control of human genes in the interest of human welfare has been made by

---

whatsoever." *The Principles of Moral and Political Philosophy*, p. 441 of the American edition of 1810.

certain sociologists and anthropologists who protest
that any scale of benefactors and malefactors is relative to the culture of the time and place, that the
genes that furthered welfare in Europe at the end of
the nineteenth century when men had trust in science and liberalism would have been deleterious in
the culture of the Dobu or Kwakiutl, and may be ineffective if not actually harmful in the civilization in
which your grandchildren will be born.

It is of course true that even superior men will act
in general accord with the customs and valuations of
their peers, and that the same human abilities and
proclivities will operate very differently for welfare
according to the spirit of the time and place. Consider a person whose genes put him high on our scale,
if born in the Europe of A.D. 100, A.D. 1100, A.D. 1500,
A.D. 1900, and A.D. 1942. This man might be, in A.D.
100, a colonial administrator taking customary tribute for Rome and less than customary emoluments
for himself, giving a better government than his district had before, using his power beneficently, and
supporting the arts and sciences of his day after the
fashion of Maecenas. The same man might, in A.D.
1100 be a feudal lord, just and merciful to his subjects, brave and wise in protecting himself and them
from attack, loyal to his lord, and faithful to the
church. In 1500 he might be a magnate of the church,
keeping his spiritual subjects on the road to heaven,
building a cathedral, encouraging educational and
agricultural progress in monasteries, controlling the
excesses of kings and lords, and helping to spread the

new learning. In 1900 he might be Andrew Carnegie, winning a great fortune by ability and energy,
giving it in some part to the community of his childhood and the city where his work was done, but
mostly in trust to aid men and women of superior
ability in their work for the welfare of mankind in
this world, believing in the freedom and tolerance of
liberalism, and trusting in progress by the thought
and work of the able and good. Or he might be
William James, or Thomas Edison, or Theodore
Roosevelt. In 2000 B.C. he might have been a medicine man or shaman wheedling his tribe by magic
threats and portents into keeping the peace within
the tribe and chipping a surplus of flints.

But genes causing intelligence and good-will were
benefactors in 2000 B.C. and probably will be in
A.D. 2000. They could do less for Europe in the dark
ages than at the acme of Roman rule. They could do
more in 1900 than in 1500, because intelligence was
freer and more esteemed, and good-will was directed
more by justice. They are doing less now because in
certain countries they are misled by pernicious doctrines and cutthroat patriotisms. We may hope that
A.D. 2000 will see a saner world.

Until we get better contributors to welfare born we
must, of course, do the best we can with people as
they are. Psychology warns against indiscriminate
help, and still more against helping most those who
will, as a result of the help, do least for the general
welfare. It is charitable to give incurables an easier
life, and even a longer life, if they desire it, but it is

equally charitable and much more advantageous for welfare to prevent industrial diseases and accidents which ruin productive workers. It is kind and noble to spend money, time, and energy in making morons a little less dull and ignorant, but it is in every way better to spend our resources in making gifted scientists, artists, and managers able to get to work for the world earlier and to do more and better work for it. Charity should begin at the top, giving first to the most promising contributors to welfare what they need to increase their powers for good. This seems axiomatic to a psychologist who knows the facts about individual differences and their causes.

But the churches and schools, and most public and private agencies for welfare, often deny it in practice if not also in principle.

Putting this principle into practice would cause almost a revolution in welfare work. It will be a most beneficent revolution, if it can be accomplished without hardening our hearts and drying up the natural springs of charity. I think it can. I will not take your time to present my reasons, but will instead quote the prophecy of Graham Wallas that the scientific study and treatment of our fellow men will deepen and broaden our love for them.

The more complex and, as one hopes, the truer description of mankind which the psychology of the twentieth century is slowly building up may help Love rather than hinder it. If, after a period of psychological reading, one stands on a railway platform or at a window, looking at that unknown crowd which makes the solitude of London, the faces which one will never see again seem less indifferent than they did before. . . . But book-learning and the habit of attention which it produces does seem to make it easier to interpret the less obvious signs of psychological states, and more probable that those states will stimulate a certain degree of Love. The tired mother snapping at her tired child, the weak smile of the dreamy youth, the intense self-consciousness of the two talkers who are "showing off" to the other inmates of the omnibus, all seem intelligible and kindly. And if formal psychology lends a measure of reality to those whom one sees only for a moment, it can also sharpen and make more poignant the mental picture, which every member of the Great Society forms, of that larger multitude of his contemporaries whom he will never see, but whose lives he must necessarily influence. . . .

The majority, however, of those who will be affected by the action of any inhabitant of a Great City or State are separate from him, not by space and multitude only, but also by time. Every ton of coal that we burn, every scar on the face of nature that we help to make, every new custom which we start or old custom which we modify, above all every act or refusal to act which affects the procreation of children, will influence the uncounted millions who do not yet exist. And perhaps the most important emotional effect of the growth and spread of psychological science may consist in such an extension of our imagination as may make more real to our feelings those in whom our type, with slow developments, must persist, even though nearly everything which now influences us after birth, may change beyond our power of prophecy.[3]

[3] From *The Great Society* by Graham Wallas, p. 154 f. By permission of The Macmillan Company, publishers.

# X

## THE PSYCHOLOGY OF WELFARE: THE
## WELFARE OF COMMUNITIES

A BILL OF SPECIFICATIONS of symptoms of a good
life for a community can be made with considerable surety that it will be acceptable to competent
thinkers. Furthermore, such a bill of specifications
can be made very largely out of items in respect to
which a community can conveniently test and measure itself, and try to improve itself.

As one step in a study of the causes of welfare, I
obtained official records of the status of over 300
cities in each of the first thirty-seven items of the
following list:

A BILL OF SPECIFICATIONS OF A GOOD LIFE
FOR A COMMUNITY

*Items 1 to 37 are the measurements used to obtain the
Thorndike G score or G index of the general goodness of
life in a city.*

*Items 38 to 43 are measurements which were not used
in the G score but could well be so used.*

*Items 44 to 46 are measurements of facts which con-
tribute to welfare, and in so far forth may be regarded as
constituents of it.*

*Items 47 to 56 are possible measurements which are
hard to make objectively and uniformly.*

*Items 57 to 72 have not as yet any demonstrably valid
objective symptoms, tests, scales or the like to measure*

*them by, but with sufficient labor and ingenuity, such should be found.*

1. Infant death-rate reversed.
2. General death-rate reversed.
3. Typhoid death-rate reversed.
4. Appendicitis death-rate reversed.
5. Puerperal diseases death-rate reversed.
6. Per capita public expenditures for schools.
7. Per capita public expenditures for teachers' salaries.
8. Per capita public expenditures for textbooks and supplies.
9. Per capita public expenditures for libraries and museums.
10. Percentage of persons sixteen to seventeen attending schools.
11. Percentage of persons eighteen to twenty attending schools.
12. Average salary of a high school teacher.
13. Average salary of an elementary school teacher.
14. Per capita public expenditures for recreation.
15. Per capita acreage of public parks.
16. Rarity of extreme poverty.
17. Rarity of less extreme poverty.
18. Infrequency of gainful employment for boys 10–14.
19. Infrequency of gainful employment for girls 10–14.
20. Average wage of workers in factories.
21. Frequency of home ownership (per capita number of homes owned).
22. Per capita support of the Y. M. C. A.
23. Excess of physicians, nurses, and teachers over male domestic servants.
24. Per capita domestic installations of electricity.
25. Per capita domestic installations of gas.
26. Per capita number of automobiles.
27. Per capita domestic installations of telephones.
28. Per capita domestic installations of radios.

29. Percent of literacy in the total population.
30. Per capita circulation of Better Homes and Gardens, Good Housekeeping, and the National Geographic Magazine.
31. Per capita circulation of the Literary Digest.
32. Death rate from syphilis (reversed).
33. Death rate from homicide (reversed).
34. Death rate from automobile accidents (reversed).
35. Per capita value of asylums, schools, libraries, museums, and parks owned by the public.
36. Ratio of the value of public property in schools, libraries, museums, and parks, etc., to the value of public property used for general government, police, etc.
37. Per capita public property minus public debt.
38. Per capita number of graduates per year from public high schools.
39. Percentage which the public expenditure for the maintenance of libraries was of the total public expenditures.
40. Per capita circulation of public libraries.
41. Per capita number of Boy Scouts.
42. Infrequency of deaths from gonococcus infections.
43. Infrequency of illegitimate births.
44. Per capita income.
45. Intelligence-test score of a fair sample of the adult population.
46. Intelligence-test score of a juvenile group old enough to be reliably tested, for example, the ten-year olds.
47. The infrequency of crimes.
48. The honesty of the local government.
49. The infrequency of venality in judges and jurors.
50. The efficiency of the local government.
51. The per capita provision by private individuals of schools, libraries, museums, parks, etc.

52. Average esthetic merit of public buildings including churches.
53. Average esthetic merit of private buildings.
54. Average esthetic merit of front yards.
55. Average esthetic merit of back yards.
56. Average esthetic merit of articles on display in shop windows.
57. Justice of race to race.
58. Justice of creed to creed.
59. Justice of majority to minority.
60. Justice of employer to employee.
61. Justice of employee to employer.
62. Justice of voters to tax-payers.
63. Justice of men to women (and vice versa).
64. Intelligent sympathy of race with race.
65. Intelligent sympathy of creed with creed.
66. Intelligent sympathy of employer with employee.
67. Intelligent sympathy of employee with employer.
68. Intelligent sympathy of old with young.
69. Intelligent sympathy of young with old.
70. Intelligent sympathy of conservative with radical.
71. Intelligent sympathy of radical with conservative.
72. Intelligent sympathy of ordinary with eccentric.

Item 23 (the excess of physicians, trained nurses, and teachers over male domestic servants) is not a regular symptom of welfare accepted by sociologists. But most of you will agree that it is better for a community to attract and support doctors, nurses, and teachers than valets, lackeys, and chauffeurs. Some of the latter doubtless serve the common good by freeing the time and energy of their masters for useful work. On the average, however, the welfare of a community will be promoted by losing ten valets and gaining ten teachers, or by losing a chauffeur and gaining a district nurse.

In this stronghold of Puritan New England, it may be argued that wide ownership of automobiles and wide ownership of radios are doubtful items, one preventing people from getting enough exercise and the other tempting them to low standards of entertainment. By personal predilection I sympathize deeply with Puritanism, but as an honest psychologist I must report that, other things being equal, the more cars and radios there are per thousand residents, the better. Cars are now about as beneficent as typewriters; these also are misused and increase the volume of annoying letters and bad novels. Listening to the radio's worst is probably better than listening to malicious village gossip.

The other items of the first 37 need no defense. Other things being equal that community is better where people live longer and have less cause to fear pestilences, where fewer mothers die in childbirth and fewer mothers lose their babies, where the citizens receive more dollars' worth of educational opportunity, where boys and girls can stay longer in school, where parks and other recreational facilities abound, where extreme poverty is less frequent, where child labor is less frequent, where factory workers are paid more, where more homes are owned, and so on.

So we use a composite score (call it G) of Items 1 to 37 as an index of the general goodness of life in a community. Items 38 to 43 are validated by common sense and also by the correspondence of scores in each of them with this G score. The measurement of such correspondence is by means of a coefficient of correlation or covariance, which may range from $+1.00$ to $-1.00$. Its meaning may be made clear by an illustration. Suppose that we had for each person in this room measurements as follows:

Height.
Weight.
Length of right forearm (from elbow to finger tip).
Length of left forearm (from elbow to finger tip).
Personal expenditures (for one's own food, clothing, rent, education, etc., etc.) in 1940.
Personal expenditures (for one's own food, clothing, rent, education, etc., etc.) in 1941.
Amount received as charity in 1940.
Amount received as charity in 1941.
Amount of food (in calories) eaten on days 1, 3, 5, 7, 9, etc. of 1940.
Amount of food eaten on days 2, 4, 6, 8, 10, etc. of 1940.

There would be a correlation of about .60 between height and weight. It would not be 1.00 because some tall persons are thin and some short persons are fat and stocky. There would be a higher correlation between height and arm length (about .80). There would be a correlation of about .95 between length of right forearm and length of left forearm. It would not be 1.00 because some of us have arms that do not correspond perfectly; when we buy clothes one sleeve has to be made somewhat longer than the other. The correlations between 1940 expenditures and 1941 expenditures would be very high. A correlation of absolutely 1.00 would be found between

1940 expenditures measured in cents and 1940 expenditures measured in dimes and fractions of a dime. The correlation between amount of food eaten on odd days in 1940 and the amount eaten on even days of 1940 would be very close to 1.00, perhaps .998. The correlation between height and expenditures would be very low, but not quite at zero, because the food and clothes for the taller persons would cost somewhat more. The correlation between height and the magnitude of the street number of the person's residence would be zero because this relation is a matter of pure chance.

The correlation between expenditures and amount received in charity would be indeterminate for the persons in this room, because few or none of you were recipients of charity. For all residents of Cambridge it would have a minus value because, for the most part, those who depended on charity had less to spend than those who did not.

Now in the 295 United States cities of from 30,000 to 500,000 population,[1] the correlations of items 38, 39, 40, etc., with G (the general goodness score computed from items 1 to 37) are all positive and substantial, being:

38 Per capita number of graduates per year from
 public high schools ............................................... .43
39 Per capita percentage which the public expenditure for the maintenance of libraries was of the total public expenditures ..................................... .54

---

[1] But with Milwaukee included and three resort cities (Atlantic City, Miami, and St. Petersburg) excluded.

40 Per capita circulation of public libraries .............. .68
41 Per capita number of Boy Scouts........................... .58
42 Infrequency of deaths from gonococcus infections .39
43 Infrequency of illegitimate births ........................ .51

In these same cities the correlation of per capita income with G score is .70.

With help from the Carnegie Corporation, Dr. Ella Woodyard and I have given a standard intelligence test to eleven thousand children sampling the population in thirty cities. I wish it could have been in three hundred. The results show that cities do differ greatly in the intelligence level of their children as measured by such tests; and that the average juvenile intelligence of a community is correlated with its G score. Adult intelligence will presumably be even more closely correlated therewith. We may then esteem intelligence not only for its own sake, but because it is one cause of welfare.

Probably all of you will admit items 47 to 51 as features of welfare in a community; and I could present evidence to support your opinion in the case of three of these items.

Items 52 to 56 are intended to measure appreciation of what is fine and free from vulgarity and ostentation. We have been able to try them out in seven cities, in which Mrs. Harford Powel and Dr. Woodyard rated adequate samples of buildings, yards, and shop-window displays. There is no difficulty save expense in obtaining a set of photographs that present an adequate and impartial report of these esthetic facts of a community. There is no difficulty save expense in having enough judges rate these photographs to provide true measures of the communities by present esthetic standards. There is no difficulty save expense in extending the data to interior decorations, women's clothes and hats, or any other visible items. There is no difficulty save expense in using sound-records to extend the data to church music, school music, and any other audible items.

Our seven cities are so small a sample that it might be wise to say nothing about the correspondence found between esthetic score and welfare score. But seven are better than none, and you may know, for what it is worth, that they show a substantial correspondence. The opinion that material prosperity and vulgarity are affiliated in communities seems contrary to the facts now, as it was in the days of Pericles in Athens and in the days of Dante in Florence.

Items 57 to 72 are inserted in recognition of the importance of inter-group justice and of intelligent tolerance and sympathy. They are not to advocate minding other people's business or being neighborly to those who wish and need to have you leave them alone. Some employees, for example, wish nothing from their employers besides high wages and good working conditions, and would not give one seed of a fig to be slapped on the back by the boss or called on by his wife. Some would.

By my methods of scoring items 1 to 37, a city that was as low in each item as the city that was the lowest of the 295 cities of 30,000 to 500,000 in that item would be given a G score of 0; a city that was as high in each item as the city that was the highest of the 295 in that item would receive a score of 1541. There could well be cities scoring 0 or even lower. There have been among Asiatic cities of the past. Cities scoring 1541 are not impossible. Indeed every city should strive to approach the composite of excellences which that score represents. The actual range in 1930 was from about 300 to about 1100.

Among the cities very high in G are: Pasadena, Montclair, Cleveland Heights, Berkeley, Brookline, and Evanston. Among those very low in G are Augusta (Ga.), Columbus (Ga.), Meridian, High Point, and Charleston (S. C.).

The scores for New England cities were: Brookline 990, Newton 890, Springfield 830, Arlington 780, Medford 780, Quincy 780, Hartford 765, Boston 750, Watertown 750, Stamford, Cambridge, Lynn, Malden, and Worcester, all year 735, New Haven 720, Everett 720, Pittsfield 705, Waltham 705, Haverhill 690, Bridgeport, New Britain, Waterbury, Portland, Revere, and Somerville all near 680, Meriden, Brockton, and Holyoke 670, Fitchburg 650, Salem and Providence 640, Cranston 625, Chelsea 610, New Bedford, Taunton, and Pawtucket 595, Fall River, Lowell, Manchester, and Nashua, all near 580, Chicopee 540, Woonsocket 520, Lewiston 440.

The welfare of a community may be defined by some reasonably weighted composite index of the items on our list, or some similar list. Welfare so defined is as real a fact as area, or rainfall, or density of population. It can be measured. Its causes can be studied.

I may note here that if the welfare of each individual in each community were measured by an index (call it B) for the degree to which he received the twenty-six blessings set forth in our bill of specification for the welfare of persons, and if the welfare measures thus obtained for all persons in a community were averaged to make an Index (Bc) we could compute the correspondence between G and Bc, that is between the welfare of a community as measured from facts about the community, and the average welfare of the persons in the community as measured by their individual welfare scores. The correlation need not be perfect; G and Bc are not two ways of measuring the same fact. It will not be perfect because many items of B (personal welfare), for example, 1, 11, 13, 16, 17, 18, 19, 22, and 23, are to a considerable degree independent of public health, schools, creature comforts, wages, and other features of G. We have, in Bc, a summation of facts about persons. We have, in G, a summation of facts about communities. Communities are in some respects more than the persons residing in them, and in some respects less. The goal of human effort should be to raise both the B scores of persons and the G scores of communities.

### THE CAUSATION OF THE WELFARE OF COMMUNITIES

For each of the 295 cities of 30,000 to 500,000 population in 1930, I gathered some three hundred items of information, including everything available that might conceivably give information concerning the causes of the great differences in welfare, as indicated by the goodness score, G.

It soon became clear that two groups of factors were very important in comparison with all others. The first group included factors relating to the per capita income of a city's residents. The second included factors relating to the intellects and characters and ideals of its residents.

We cannot obtain direct measurements of the number of dollars of each person's income in these cities and compute per capita income by simple arithmetic. But we can obtain fairly dependable measures which would parallel such direct measures of per capita income if they were available, by using a reasonably weighted average of the following items:

| Item | Approximate Weight |
|---|---|
| Per capita number of income-tax returns of $2,-500 or more (average of 1930 and 1931) | 15 |
| Per capita number of income-tax returns of incomes exceeding $5,000 (estimated from the data for counties) | 7 |
| Average salary of high-school teachers plus average salary of elementary-school teachers | 3 |
| Average salary of full-time employees in all retail stores | 5 |
| Average wage in manufacturing plants | 6 |
| Average rental (or equivalent in case of homes owned) | 3 |
| Per capita sales of retail food stores | 4 |

Per capita sales of cigar stores ............................. 1
Per capita sales of drug stores ............................ 1

Let us call this index of per capita income I and observe the correlation or correspondence between I and G, the index of welfare or the general goodness of life. It is close, not only in these 295 large cities, but also in the 159 cities of from 20,000 to 30,000 inhabitants, and in the 48 states. I and whatever it involves has presumably a substantial influence on G.

The group of items related to the personal qualities of a city's residents included the following:

| Item | Approximate Weight |
|---|---|
| Per capita number of graduates from public high schools in 1934 | 1½ |
| Percentage which public expenditures for the maintenance of libraries was of the total public expenditures | ¾ |
| Percentage of illiteracy (reversed) | ⅞ |
| Percentage of illiteracy among those aged 15–24 (reversed) | 1 |
| Per capita circulation of public libraries | 1⅔ |
| Per capita number of homes owned | 1½ |
| Per capita number of physicians, nurses and teachers minus male domestic servants | 1¼ |
| Per capita number of telephones | 1 |
| Number of male dentists divided by number of male lawyers | ⅔ |
| Per capita number of deaths from syphilis (reversed) | 1 |
| Per capita number of deaths from homicide (reversed) | 1 |

Let us call a composite score in which the relative weights are as shown above, P. The P scores of the cities, and also of the states, correspond with the G scores even more closely than the I or income scores do.

The I and P scores together account for three quarters of the variation among cities in G score.

To be exact, the variation in welfare as measured by G is determined as follows:
In the 295 large cities:

26½ hundredths by what is measured by I and not by P
43   hundredths by what is measured by P and not by I
 4½ hundredths by what is common to I and P (call it $\overline{IP}$)
26   hundredths by what is not measured by I, P, or $\overline{IP}$

In 144 cities of 20,000 to 30,000 residents:

22½ hundredths by what is measured by I and not by P
43   hundredths by what is measured by P and not by I
17   hundredths by what is common to I and P (call it $\overline{IP}$)
17½ hundredths by what is not measured by I, P, or $\overline{IP}$

In the 48 states:

14   hundredths by what is measured by I and not by P
46   hundredths by what is measured by P and not by I
23½ hundredths by what is common to I and P (call it $\overline{IP}$)
16½ hundredths by what is not measured by I, P, or $\overline{IP}$

The unidentified something that is common to I and P is presumably an aggregation of qualities like industry, honesty, and certain features of intelligence which make persons earn more as well as learn to read and write, reach high grades in schools, and avoid syphilis and murder.

The recipe for the welfare of a community is, in so

far forth, very simple. Put able and good people in the community and provide them with high incomes. Nothing else is comparable to these in importance.

Some of you may be mystified by the sudden transition from measures of correlation or covariance to statements about determination or causation, and even a bit skeptical. I may seem to have pulled the causes of welfare out of a table of correlation coefficients as a magician pulls rabbits out of an empty hat. The abrupt transition was to spare you a discussion of the techniques of partial correlation, multiple correlation, and path coefficients. We cannot make cities in a laboratory with specified amounts of I and P and $\overline{IP}$, the unidentified something which is common to I and P, and watch the results of increasing I without changing P, P without changing I, etc. But we can isolate the influence of each of these factors by proper methods of analysis of correlations.[2]

If I had dependable measures of the intelligence, good-will, kindness, honesty, love of family, industry, prudence, etc., etc., of the residents in each of the cities and states, I could proceed to measure, within P or beneath P, the contribution that each of these characteristics of the population makes to welfare

[2] It may be noted also that if all items that are constituents of I or of P are subtracted from G, the causation of the variation in the new G that remains is substantially the same as before. No genuine features of welfare should be subtracted from G, however, merely because they are also features of per capita income or of the personal qualities of residents. There is nothing spurious in what they contribute to the correlations.

independently of all the others. For the present, P is defined only by the measures that constitute it, but all competent students will expect that it is some aggregation of personal qualities of the population, and mainly of qualities of intellect and character.

Consider now some of the features of a community that do *not* cause welfare, and especially some that may surprise you.

Size is unimportant for welfare. Its obvious advantages are balanced by less obvious disadvantages.

Wealth, as measured by the per capita value of taxable property, has no influence upon welfare, except as it increases the per capita income.

The distribution of wealth and income seems to have no relation to welfare except as it influences, or is a symptom of, P, the personal-qualities score. As a rough but impartial measure of the amount of inequality in wealth and income we may use the spread of amounts paid for rental (or suitable equivalents in the case of owned homes). For example, New Haven and Loraine had the same median rental, but in New Haven a spread of $167.00 was required to include 90 per cent of the rentals, whereas in Loraine the spread was only $96. The 95 percentile rental was nearly 1200 per cent of the 5 percentile rental in New Haven and only about 650 per cent thereof in Loraine.

Those cities where the inequality in rentals is greatest are lower in G than the rest, but only because their P scores are lower. So far as the facts for our 295 cities go, the following statements are true:

It is bad for a city to have many poor people, and, other things being equal, the poorer they are the worse it is. But it is good for a city to have many rich people, and, other things being equal, the richer they are the better. Cities with a wide spread in rentals are better in G than cities with a narrower spread, but this is mainly because a wider spread of rentals goes with a higher average per capita income. Cities with high ratios of 95 percentile or 90 percentile rentals to 5 percentile or 10 percentile rentals are worse in G than cities with low ratios, but this is mainly because high rental ratios go with low scores in P.[3]

Giving equal weight to the spread and the ratio, and allowing for the linkages with I and P, the influence of the distribution of income as shown in rentals is approximately zero.[4]

In and of itself equality in the distribution of wealth or income has no appreciable influence in

[3] It is not hard to see why communities high in P should have lower ratios of the 95 percentile or 90 percentile rentals to the 5 percentile or 10 percentile rentals than communities low in P have. There are fewer poor people; those that there are spend less on vice and folly and more on their homes and families. There are more rich people, but these are probably less prodigal and ostentatious.

[4] The correlations for the 295 cities are:

Variability in rentals with G, −.24
Variability in rentals with I,   .23
Variability in rentals with P, −.51
G with I, .72   G with P, .80   I with P, .39

The partial correlation of variability in rentals with G in cities alike in I and P is consequently −.13.

making one city's G score higher than another's. Among cities equally good in P, differences in the amount of income per thousand residents are important, but differences in how it is distributed have little or no importance.

The wise things for a community to do about private wealth are to increase it in forms that will increase income and to guard it against depredation and waste. The wise things for a community to do about income are to increase it, to improve the personal qualities of residents rich and poor who will then use what they get more for the common good, to make sure that what is taken from the rich in taxes is spent so as to do more for the common good than would have been done if it had been left at the disposal of those who acquired it lawfully, and not to indulge in any schemes of equalizing income for equality's sake.

One of the commonest opinions about the welfare of communities is that factory towns and cities are near the bottom of the scale. With your permission I will quote what I have written elsewhere on this matter.

Literary men have almost universally berated the factory town as a dull, unhappy and sordid place. But they have probably attached too much weight to its appearance from the outside. The fields and cottages of agricultural laborers are more attractive to look at than the tenements of a factory city, but perhaps not to live in. Fresh air is not comforting to a man who has not enough to eat; and the beauties of nature are less entertaining to most people than human action and social intercourse.

Social reformers found an easy mark for attack in the inhuman treatment of children in the early factories of the nineteenth century, and are still extremely antagonistic to factory work for women and children and critical of it for anybody. But they compare the life of a factory city rather with an ideal of life for working people than with the lives the residents would have had if they had stayed on the farms of this country and Europe whence they came. . . .

Nobody has a good word for the manufacturing cities. This is partly prejudice. We acclaim the irrigation of a desert, but not the building of a factory, yet the benefits are much alike. We are more obviously illogical when we welcome the construction of a dam to furnish power, and grow lyrical over the lessening of housewives' labor by the use of the power in vacuum cleaners and electric refrigerators, but lament the use of the power to make them! We let the evils of the factory blind us to its good.

I must say a good word for the factory city, for, whatever my personal feelings may be, the correlations with G declare that factory cities are no worse than the general run. The correlation for the number of factory workers per thousand population is $-.01$, and by any reasonable allowances for the age-composition of the populations of the cities, it will rise above zero.[5]

As a fifth shock to common opinions about the causes of differences among communities in welfare, consider the facts about church membership. There is no evidence that a high percentage of church members increases welfare. The correlation with G is in fact slightly negative ( $-.22$ for all the cities and

[5] E. L. Thorndike, *Your City* (1939), pp. 87–89, slightly modified. Quoted by permission of the publishers, Harcourt, Brace and Company, New York.

−.20 if suburban cities and cities of the Old South are omitted). A high percentage of church membership is affiliated with typical features of traditional personal morality, its correlations with homicide, deaths from venereal diseases, and illegitimate births being −.30, −.28 and −.12½; but it is not affiliated with the broader aspects of a desirable citizenship represented in our index P. Allowance for the linkages between church membership and percentage of negroes, percentage of foreign-born, age distribution within the city, and other variables will not raise these correlations above zero. This may not surprise you as much as it did me, since almost all of you are of a generation to whom the church means much less as a civilizing agency than it did a half century ago. You may be ready to believe that the churches now are clubs of estimable people and maintainers of traditional rites and ceremonies rather than powerful forces for human betterment. Unless there are mysterious forces which cause the better communities to under-report their church membership and the worse communities to over-report theirs, we must believe something like that.

Consider now some possible causes of welfare, in addition to I and P.

The first is the P scores of the residents one generation, or two generations, ago. So far as they influenced the genes, and also the customs and ideals of the present generation the P of 1900 and the P of 1870 are represented in our P of 1930. But in so far as they taxed themselves to buy parks, build schools,

and reduce public debt, or saved and invested so as
to provide income for future generations, past generations may improve the present G in other ways
than via the present P.

Unfortunately the P of 1870 and the P of 1900
cannot be measured, and one can do little better
than guess at the amount of their influence on the G
of 1930. My guess is that the P of 1900 has some
independent influence, but less than a tenth of that
of the P of 1930. In my opinion, a community cannot
live much or long on its past. As actual evidence I
have only the facts for a composite of per capita
value of public property minus public debt and per
capita value of public property in schools, parks, etc.,
two items which are specially due to previous generations in many cities. This composite makes a
positive, though small, contribution.

Another possible cause of welfare is such natural
physical resources as harbor, river frontage, water
power, climate, and proximity to fertile lands or rich
mines. When estimated impartially though rather
crudely for each city, natural advantages showed
very little relation to welfare. But the matter is
complicated by the fact that residential suburbs like
Brookline, White Plains, Haverford, Oak Park, or
Evanston, which are very high in G score, have less
than average natural advantages, but are in some
ways parasitic upon the large cities which they ad-
join. The matter needs further study with more accurate estimates of natural advantages.

There is some reason to believe that homogeneity

of the population in respect of color, race, religious denomination, and the like helps welfare a little.

In spite of careful investigation of the facts generally available about the governments of these cities, and of letters to all the mayors asking for certain facts not available in print, I cannot inform you how much better a commission or city-manager government is for welfare than old-fashioned governments as by alderman and a common council. Nor can I inform you how much harm inefficiency and graft do. I can only throw up a few statistical straws to show how the wind blows.

I have made a composite measure of the reported extent to which each city spent money (per capita) for city planning, vital statistics, civil service examinations, public convenience stations, and probation systems. The reversed death-rates for homicide and typhoid are perhaps indications of goodness of local government in preventing crime and pestilence, and I have made a composite of them giving equal weight to each. Putting these two composites together with equal weight we have a measure (call it GOV) which does add something not already in I or P to the causation of G. Something, but not much. It is very unlikely that even a perfect measure of differences in goodness of government would add more than five hundredths to the 80 or more hundredths of the variation in G that I and P account for.

The largest actual addition to the causation that I have been able to demonstrate is by improving the personal-qualities score (P) by adding a $P_1$, consisting of per capita illegitimate births and deaths from venereal diseases other than syphilis (reversed in both cases).

Using I, P, this $P_1$, the composite of items 35 and 37, the GOV composite, and an indication of the physical health of the population consisting of the general death-rate and infant death-rate reversed, the total fraction of the variation in G accounted for is .91, the multiple correlation being .953. I leave to some ambitious social psychologist among you the task of accounting for the nine hundredths still undetermined.[6]

[6] Very likely there will be more than nine hundredths to account for. My procedures in selecting these additional possible causes of welfare involved trying many and retaining those which seemed reasonable and also did in fact increase the multiple correlation. This is permissible but risky; and a prudent scientist will try to check such multiple correlations by an independent set of observations. Unfortunately, the data for P and Gov were not available for the 144 cities of 20,000 to 30,000 residents, or for the forty-eight states.

# INDEX

# INDEX